Love Without Conditions

by

Rodney R. Romney

*The more man becomes man, the more will he become prey to
a need, a need that is always more explicit, more subtle and
more magnificent, the need to adore.*

—*Pierre Teilhard de Chardin*

Riverrun Press
New York

Also by Rodney R. Romney
A Promise of Light
Journey To Inner Space

To obtain additional copies,
please send $6.95 plus $1.75 shipping
($.50 shipping for each additional book)
New York sales tax where applicable
and mail to:

Riverrun Press
P. O. Box 367
Piermont, NY 10968

Cover and Book Design by Donna Schwartz
Typeset in Bookman by ETCetera ENTerprises, Congers, NY
Produced in the U. S. A. by Riverrun Press, Piermont, NY

ISBN 0-936415-01-0

*Special thanks to my secretary,
Beth Russell,
for her faithful assistance as typist,
and to Barbara Deal
for her editing and
many helpful suggestions.*

Contents

Introduction

This is a book about love, the universal destiny of all humanity. It is also a book about God, the Creator of the universe and the One whose nature is to love. As such, it tackles two immense and seemingly impossible subjects. Much talk about love is notoriously sentimental, and much talk about God is notoriously confusing. While I cannot totally avoid the sentimental aspect of love, I do hope to avoid making the notion of God any more confusing that it already is.

This is a book about a certain kind of love, a love that has no conditions before it can operate, a love that is freeing rather than restricting, a love that is universal rather than exclusive, a love that is as essential to our being as nourishment and rest are to our bodies. It is this love for which the heart of humanity hungers. Indeed, all creation is united in a cry for this love. Until we find it, we are in exile from our true selves and our greatest happiness.

We spend our lives searching for this love but do not always know what it is we are seeking nor where to turn to find it. This book seeks to define our search and to point in some directions that will help us find the thing which all our lives we have craved. I make no claims here beyond the claim of love itself, for these pages were forged from that crucible of love which has gradually and inexorably become a part of my own life. Not that I claim to model this love perfectly. I fail in more instances than I care to confess. But I know that love without conditions has been given to me, so it is possible. More than possible, it is absolutely imperative.

We live in confusing times. People who talk of "limited nuclear war" and of national security through Star Wars defenses in space are often heralded as the realists of our age, while those of us who speak of unconditional love and global peace are labeled impractical and deluded. Yet despair has never been more powerful or prevalent than it is today. Belief is widespread that love is a sentimental delusion and peace an impossible dream.

It is my deepest conviction that love is the most dynamic concept of our lives. It is a condition of life and the fundament of all human rights. It is not only a right, it is a duty, for from love spring the fruits of peace and justice. It is unconditional love that will empower us to feel and take personal responsibility for the development of our planet, rather than standing by and watching its annihilation.

As our twentieth century rolls to an end, we are being called upon to face, in all their tragic urgency, the personal needs of each of us, the common needs of all humanity, and the needs of all created species. This book is for those who want to enlarge their love in order to create a new reality, a reality of a world that Jesus Christ described as the Kingdom of Heaven. As the word spreads that unconditional love is not only desirable but possible, world consciousness will shift. We will abandon our hair-trigger balance of terror and offer a new legacy to our children, a legacy which will reaffirm the basic spiritual nature of humankind and which will bring us home to the true nature of our being—a love without conditions.

Chapter One

Many Kinds Of Love

God is love. And since God is an infinite being, God is love on an infinite level. No matter what other adjectives and descriptions we assign to God, they all come back to the same thing. God is love, and nothing but love.

You are love. And so am I. We are love because we have been created in the image and likeness of God. No matter what other assessments and determinations we make about ourselves, we are brought back to the inescapable fact of our being, made true by our birthright. We are love and nothing but love.

This love of God and our own love are one and the same thing, and this is a love which can never be extinguished. Whether we make our bed in the depths of despair, or descend into the pits of depravity, that love is there. It cannot be extinguished, any more than you and I can be extinguished, for that love is eternal and the sole reason for our existence.

In our being, and in our yearnings, and in our strivings and in all our motions, we retain the remembrance of God from whom we have come. This God has become incarnate in us by love and in such a way that we can love ourselves and love others and love millions of souls we have never met, simply by drawing on that love. We are a creation of love, and we have been created to love. When that love is denied or impeded in its flow, we become less than ourselves, less than human, less than whole.

In our times of loneliness and lostness, it was love that found us and brought us home. In our days of grief and bewilderment, it was love that came to us and dried our tears. In our journeys through the dark night of shadow and the valley of peril, it was love that rescued us and set us on a better path. We owe our existence to love, for love is the reason we are here. We must give ourselves wholly to this love and allow it to flow through us into all the world. We are the transmitters of the highest and the holiest energy known to humankind. We are not only the givers and the bearers of love, we are love itself.

God loves us individually and not just collectively. God loves us much more than we love ourselves. That love is often unrequited. We try to spurn it, turn our backs on it, run from it, and this is a great tragedy for God, but a greater tragedy for us. Yet God is always entreating us in love to come back, to make our home in the heart of his divine being, to give ourselves unresistingly to him, that God may give Godself to us in greater and fuller measure.

God's love is a love without conditions. We do nothing to earn it, and we can do nothing to destroy it. There are, however, certain conditions necessary to make this love fully operative. We have to recognize it and want it, and we must be willing to share it with others. We cannot hoard it or keep it for ourselves. When we fulfill these basic requirements, then our lives blossom, our fears and anxieties diminish, and God begins to dwell in us to share his unconditional love with the world.

This book is a journey of love. It is an exploration into love without conditions. It asks only two things of you: an open mind and an open heart. When the mind is open, truth will flourish. When the heart is open, love will blossom. When the mind and the heart are both open, then the soul is open. God will then appear in the glory of this unconditional love.

The ancient Greeks were wise enough to know that love is too complex to be encompassed in a single word. They had at least three words which broke down the basic components of love in three categories: erotic love, familial love, and a third kind of love which they called agape. Traditional theology said this third kind was divine love, holy love, God's love. It is agape love that I equate with unconditional love.

Divine love is love without conditions. You can't do anything to earn it. It is a free gift of God's grace. Yet in order for the gift to be received it must first be accepted and then shared as widely as possible. This divine love not only seeks to generate such responses, it impinges upon every other kind of love. In fact, all other loves spring from divine love. As the scriptures point out, "We love because God first loved us."

Yet love, like any other emotion or quality, can get out of balance or become perverted from the purity of its source. Like a spring bubbling forth its pure waters, this love is perfect at its source. But just as pure water can become contaminated, so pure love can become corrupted. When there is no more infilling of the spring from its deep and hidden source, it becomes stagnant and eventually dries up. When love becomes separated from its deep and hidden source, which is God, it branches off into lesser and often destructive forms of love. Separation from God, the fount of unconditional love, is the cause of all human problems.

Leo Buscaglia speaks of love as a learned phenomenon, rather than something that lies dormant in each human being. While it is true that love is learned, it is also true that love lives potentially in all of us. It is also true, as Buscaglia suggests, that love is not something we learn in our present education system. We learn to love by being loved. How we learn love is then determined initially by the home and culture in which we grew.

I grew up in a home where love was somewhat fragmented yet never totally lacking. My mother and father were divorced by the time I had barely learned to walk. Both my parents were absent from my life for long periods of time when I was young. My mother worked to support my two older brothers and me, and my father retreated to a hermit-like existence in the mountains as a mining prospector. I never doubted that my parents loved me, but I yearned for love to be more present, more solidified. Consequently, I entered my teens a shy, sensitive person, unsure whether to take any risks in claiming love and friendship from others.

When I was not quite sixteen, I experienced God's love in a strong dramatic fashion. It happened in a revival service in a little Baptist church in rural Idaho, where, at the moment of yielding myself to the call of the preacher to come forward and accept Jesus Christ, I felt a love of the most indescribable dimensions I had ever known. For those few moments, as I made the journey down that church aisle, I was consumed by a love that brought all the lost and lonely pieces of my being into place, suspended me, as it were, above the reach of fear, doubt or insecurity, and merged past, present and future in such a way that mortal time was temporarily transcended.

The years following that experience had much to teach me about God's love. But it is doubtful that I would have been open to such teaching if I had not had that mystical moment of awareness where I knew I was loved, absolutely and unconditionally, just as I was, with no strings or requirements attached.

Therefore, I say love cannot be learned until it is received as the free and valuable gift it is. All our theorizing about love will never produce love in our lives. That only comes when someone loves us. Moreover, while love is more than a feeling, love can never be present where feeling is absent.

Pierre Teilhard de Chardin, a French Jesuit priest and paleontologist, called love the most universal, the most tremendous and the most mysterious of the cosmic forces. He said that efforts of the social institutions to dyke and canalize love, or attempts of the moralist to get it to submit to rules, have only made it more wild and ungoverned. Teilhard defined love in its essence as the attraction exercised on each unit of consciousness by the center of the universe in course of taking shape. He described it as the primal and universal psychic energy which only reveals its secrets and its virtues when it becomes "hominized."[1]

Teilhard was a complex and brilliant thinker. If I understand him correctly at this point, he was suggesting that prior to the appearance of the human species, love was divergent, resulting in the production of an ever-increasing number and variety of living forms. In humans, however, love became convergent. Love acquired a moral character because humans were able to love God consciously, the first species of the created order to do so. The whole purpose of love being hominized in this way was to make preparation for the Christ and the total transformation of the planet. This hominization of love has an evolutionary aspect and points the way to a future where love will be deliberately fused with the natural sap of the universe. At that point we will succeed in consummating a union with the universe by simultaneously sharing a union with all the men and women who inhabit our planet.

The hominization of love, or the idea of the Word becoming flesh, raises for us the question of the relationship of physical or material love to spiritual love. The two are so interconnected and intertwined that it is sometimes impossible to say where one leaves off and the other begins. High peak experiences of divine love do seem to transcend the physical, and yet the body is still the agent through which the experience comes.

A young woman once came to a counselor because of her inability to separate the physical from the spiritual. She was a sensitive, caring person, taking on the burdens and concerns of others with a kind of instinctive compassion. Her concern for those who were afflicted with the burdens and problems of life had increased to the point where there was almost nothing she would not do to help. As might be expected, others began to take advantage of her, for she had very little protection. Her love made her a vulnerable target. To her chagrin, she became sexually involved with several men she had attempted to befriend. Her zeal to be an unbounded and continuous channel of helping love was somehow deceived and perverted into a temporary attraction on the material plane. She grew increasingly confused and unsettled over the distinctions between sexuality and spirituality. More accurately, she failed to see the cosmic role of sexuality in its full breadth. Her desire to be helpful to others needed to be brought into a coherence with a vaster realm of reality. Once this was pointed out to her, she began to work on utilizing her compassion in more constructive forms.

So close is the link between sexuality and spirituality that, as I have said, it is easily possible to confuse one for the other. Indeed, sexuality in its finest form is spiritual. But not until we succeed in keeping these two forms in balance can we really go on and explore the wider dimensions of unconditional love. Sexuality is meant to be an exchange between two people, based on an exclusive commitment. Shared with one person it can merge into the true upward union of spirits, but shared with many or even with several simultaneously, it dissolves into an energy that sucks up unto itself, rather than becoming a transforming kind of energy. It is important for us to understand this distinction early, for failure to recognize the thin and often invisible line that divides materiality from spirituality will corrupt our pursuit of unconditional love and eventually bring about failure.

Once when I was leading a ministers' retreat, I asked the conferees to share their two greatest fears. A few ministers found it impossible to do this. After all, ministers are chosen by God and not supposed to have fears. But several ministers, who knew better than that, were honest in admitting that their two greatest fears were fear of failure and fear of being alone.

I think these are the overriding fears that haunt most of us. We are so achievement oriented in this world that we fear we will not succeed where we ought. That fear feeds into our fear of being alone. If we fail (ourselves, others, God) we think we will be abandoned.

Jesus said that perfect love casts out fear. His point is aptly made. If we know ourselves to be loved perfectly and completely and know that love is not based on any conditions, such as success or failure, that it will never be taken from us, no matter what, then our greatest fears disappear. Unconditional love sets us free from our fears and enables us to go on and explore the dimensions of this love that is always seeking to invade our lives with its warm and penetrating light.

Everyone in your world at this moment—your parents, your mate, your siblings, your friends—loves you with the same love and yet a love which is very different in its aspects. No two persons ever love us in exactly the same way. There are as many kinds of love in your world as there are persons loving you. Yet this love springs from the same source, God. Therefore, all love holds the potential of being unconditional.

If we are willing to make more room in our lives for God and take on the attitudes which are necessary for that to happen, we shall experience love of a greater quality and quantity than any we have known. We shall discover how deeply and completely God loves each of us, and in that discovery we shall be freer to love others in a more total way.

The future lies in the hands of those who are able to give the next generation good reason to love. This will be the "credo" of our search through the pages of this book. I hope it will also become the "credo" of our lives.

---

[1] Teilhard de Chardin, Pierre. **Human Energy.** Trans. J. M. Cohen. New York: Harcourt Brace Jovanovich, Inc., 1962, 32-34.

Chapter Two

Towards A Theology Of Unconditional Love

The New Testament encourages us to face life with the conviction that "God is able to make all grace abound." What God offers us is a fellowship of eternally outgoing love. We believe that creation is a delight to God and that its main function is related to the development and enjoyment of God forever. We also believe that creation needs to be completed or transformed in accord with this new state of fellowship. As Nels F.S. Ferre, a seminary/ university professor, has said, "God is the loving parent who has no permanent problem children."[2] God has children who have problems, and some of those children have become temporary problems to themselves and others, but ultimately God will redeem and control that which God has created.

How different this world would be today if we had really trusted the above to be true and not surrendered this truth to traditional faith as it developed in the early centuries following Christ. Either God is absolute, unconditional love, or God is not. Either God will have complete and total victory over creation, or God will have no victory at all. If God is unconditional, absolute love, then the questions as to our future and the outcome of this world is settled. *Unconditional love will win unconditional surrender from all that love has created.* God will rule everywhere and forever. Creation's divine purposes will be consummated.

It has been said that the law of gravity represents the continual effort of the universe to straighten itself out. Likewise, the law of unconditional love represents the continual effort of God to redeem creation, to get it straightened out. Some might say at this point that the law of gravity is unbreakable, whereas the law of love is broken all the time. In truth, the law of love cannot be broken. We can break ourselves by throwing ourselves against it and be refusing to accept it and live by it. But the law of love, like the law of gravity, remains inviolate. It cannot be broken, and ultimately it must be obeyed.

What then will happen to us, since obviously the world is not living by the law of love? Will God eventually force us into line by coercion or determination? No. If this had been the case, the world would not be in the state it is in today and humans would have long ago surrendered their freedom of choice. But God will ultimately direct our choices by making the condition of love such a desired direction that we will finally surrender to it. We will see that to go any other way is to go against our own true good.

As Shakespeare wisely said in **Hamlet,** "There is divinity that shapes our ends, rough-hew them how we will." We might paraphrase him and say, "There is a love that is always working on our behalf, not to overrule our own authority or to override our freedom of choice, but to help us use our authority wisely and make our choices carefully."

Some may accuse me here of offering a drug to an already drug-sodden humanity, deluding them about God's judgment and the final destiny of errant human beings who fall under the wrath of divine judgement. Let me speak, therefore, to the idea of salvation and the ideas of judgment that usually accompany it.

There is no mechanistic way to salvation. Mouthing certain formulae or espousing belief in certain doctrines does not meet the conditions of salvation. But there are conditions for salvation which God has set forth, and these must be met. They are as necessary as the very nature of God. The major condition is that we accept the love that God offers and be willing to share this love with others.

The parable that Jesus told about the sheep being separated from the goats (Matthew 25:31-46), one being sent into eternal punishment and the other into eternal life, says nothing about right or wrong beliefs. It all has to do with how one treats another. The Kingdom of Heaven, says Jesus, belongs to those who feed the hungry, give drink to the thirsty, welcome to the strangers, clothing to the naked, healing to the sick, and companionship to the imprisoned. Whether one is even conscious that these deeds are salvific is immaterial, says Jesus, for "inasmuch as you did it to one of the least of these, you did it to me."

Does this mean, then, that salvation is by good works and not faith? No. It means that the basic requirement of salvation has to do with love. God lays down no dogmatic rules of belief. God lays down only the rule of love without conditions. The arms of God are ever open, the heart of God is ever loving. God will not, to be sure, go after us and force us to come to him, any more than the father would go after the prodigal son in the parable (Luke 15:11-32). But when the son finally comes to his senses and realizes that his separation from the father is really his death, and when he decides in faith to go back home, then the father is there to meet him, bestowing forgiveness even before it is requested and restoring all the treasures that the son thought he had forfeited forever.

When the psalmist cried, "He restoreth my soul," he knew that only God has the capacity to do that. God is both the creator and the restorer of the human soul.

The length of the salvation road none of us can measure, nor is it up to us to determine who is on it and who is not. We are all in various stages of being in a far country or else making our way back home to the heart of God. It is, therefore, futile to make assessments about who is or is not saved. Salvation is a way and not a state, a journey and not an arrival.

God is immeasurably kind, encouraging us as we journey and helping us make the best choices, instead of judging us because of our mistakes. Why should it make us angry that this is so? Why should we Christians, like the older brother in the parable of the prodigal son, the one who stayed home, resent the fact that God's loving favor is also bestowed on the errant and wayward ones? Should we not instead rejoice that we have a God of such magnanimous and far-reaching compassion?

Nels Ferre said that it is not necessary to know the historic Jesus in order for God's will and way to be accepted, and that the eternal God is not exhausted nor totally defined by the historic Jesus.[3] It was a bold, disturbing statement. Yet if one can sense a distinction between the Jesus of history and the Christ of God, such thinking might become more palatable.

God's gracious purpose in Jesus the Christ is the fullest activity of God we can know. But though that purpose was conclusively expressed in the historic Jesus, it was not exclusively limited to him. We are saved by accepting the Christ, not by idolizing or worshipping an historic human personality. When Jesus is moved over into the place of God, we have a form of idolatry. Jesus came to show us God and said that was his primary reason for coming. He did not come to show himself. He did not invite others to worship him; he invited them to worship God. God was in Jesus, but Jesus himself was not the eternal God. He was the Son of God, the Word of God dwelling in human flesh. The Christ who became flesh in Jesus, the cosmic Christ who transcends time and division and who is present wherever God is worshipped, whether verbalized or not, is the Christ we must accept before there can be salvation. My argument with fundamentalist Christians is not that they make too much out of Jesus Christ but that they make too little. The idea of the cosmic Christ eludes the narrow, dogmatic views of far too many.

In the past, the Word has taken on the flesh of many

enlightened beings. This is more proof of the universal love God has for all human beings. We should not lay down any rules that would limit the freedom of God. The final destiny of everyone is to be with God forever and to share fellowship with God throughout all eternity. This is a staggering truth, almost too vast and overwhelming for us to accept and assimilate. Nevertheless, it is so. Whatever unconditional love may be, it needs no compelling logic to verify it. Truth, as we know it, consists in the conformity of things to the eternal Word of God, so that the truth of every created thing is evident only in the light of God.

Millions of highly intelligent people find no grounds for believing in God, and they do not believe. But everyone has a compelling need to love and be loved. Behind this need stands God, who has planted his own best argument for his existence in the heart of each of his children. The fact that we all yearn to be loved, and that we also yearn for a place to bestow our love, is proof of the fact that a common thread has been woven through all creation. That thread, the thread of love, is leading us to our final destiny, a place where we shall all together find and do the holy will of God.

Some might ask how this notion of unconditional love is verified by the Bible, so let me address that concern.

There are traces of unconditional love in the Old Testament, but these are often hidden under a heavy overlay of traditions about God's judgment and anger against an unfaithful and rebellious people, the Israelites. From the Christian perspective, the matter is settled by the New Testament. It is here we meet the unconditional love of God as the very heart of the gospel.

The New Testament, however, as Ferre points out, has more than one strain or tradition on this subject. It is not always clear, and the discerning student must understand the various traditions and then select the one that he or she wishes to follow. This selection must always be made on what tradition is believed to be the most congruent with the central message of Jesus Christ.

One persistent teaching in the New Testament is that the sinner will perish. This has been termed as the doctrine of conditional immortality. Thinkers within many denominations and traditions hold to this view. The difficulty with this view, says biblical scholar George A. Gordon, is that it sunders the solidarity of humankind. There is a greater difficulty than that. It makes God less than sovereign and all-powerful. Evil is such a problem in the world that God has had to give up on a portion of creation, according to this doctrine.

What happens to those on whom God gives up? One view is that God incinerates them in a place called hell. Here they are sent to burn forever in everlasting torment. Another view is that death is the manner in which God liquidates them, rather than consigning them to a place of eternal hell. They simply go to sleep and awaken no more. Hence, the term conditional immortality. They did not fulfill the conditions required to become immortal.

There are several obvious problems with the doctrine of conditional immortality. First of all, it is abhorrent! It is impossible to think of an earthly father or mother treating their children in this manner, let alone a Heavenly One. It makes no allowances for those who have never in this life had a chance to hear the gospel, and it imposes grave doubts on the sovereignty of God. A God who could bring this marvelous creation into being, but who is then unable to redeem and sustain it, can hardly be called a God at all. Moreover, such thinking leads to smug assumptions and complacent superiority on the part of those individuals or groups who consider themselves the saved or the in-group.

To a certain degree, this doctrine is more dependent upon specific traditions and a kind of external biblicism than it is upon the New Testament itself. To be sure, the Bible does talk about an eternal hell. But the idea of eternity as an everlasting line of time was not a Hebrew or Greek concept. It simply meant "for a long time" rather than "for all time." Eternal life in biblical thinking had to do with quality of life rather than quantity.

Where God is absent, life is a place of hell. The word "hell" is from an old English verb meaning "to be walled off" or "to be shut apart." To be "helled" was to be separated from God or from one's earthly companions. This is not far from the idea behind the New Testament meaning of the word hell, but that meaning was never intended to convey foreverness. In the New Testament the English word "hell" was translated from the Aramaic word "Gehenna," which was the name of a garbage dump outside the city of Jerusalem where a fire was always kept burning for the sake of sanitation. When Jesus used the word in his teachings, it was obviously allegorical, meaning when our sins have separated us from God, there is a fire burning in our spirits which is ultimately meant to purify and restore us to our original divine image. Hell is not a place where we go for what we did or did not do, or did or did not believe. Hell is a state of consciousness that comes about when we have willfully separated ourselves from God or part of God's beloved creation.

Some people prefer to believe that the New Testament teaches eternal hell. To do this, they must ignore nearly all forms of modern biblical scholarship, and they must also ignore another strain of thought or tradition which is prevalent in the scriptures. The Bible also teaches that God's mercy is everlasting and that love never fails.

This leads us then to a third tradition in the New Testament, which is this: *God in Christ will have sovereign victory over all in terms of his own love.* There are numerous verses that speak of this: "Every knee shall bow and tongue confess that Jesus Christ is Lord"; "God has shut up all into disobedience, that he might have mercy upon all"; "God so loved the world, that he gave his only Son . . . that the world through him might be saved." Jesus Christ is consistently referred to as the Savior of all men and women, and we are told that even if we are faithless, God will be faithful, for God cannot deny himself.

Competent Bible scholars like C.H. Dodd, Nels Ferre, and Karl Barth, find strong universalism in the Bible, both in the teachings of Jesus and the writings of Paul. These men argue that the total message of the New Testament is that God would have all to be saved and that with God all things are possible.

I opt for this line of thinking. It seems to me that the total logic of the Bible is forthright and irrefutable at this point. God can and will effect the total victory of unconditional love. Nothing that can happen will ultimately change God's love or upset God's plans. Everything will eventually be made subservient to God. Those who worship the sovereign God dare proclaim nothing less than the total victory of God's unconditional love. No other position can be consistently Christian.

This is not meant to ignore the fact that humans need to be converted to this love. The Bible presents us with a true picture of ourselves—weak and failing creatures who need God. To ignore this aspect of the human condition would be to rob the gospel of its realism and to deny God's love the power of its effectiveness. God's love is not conditioned by human behavior. It is constant and unchanging, and it is ever seeking to woo us beyond the levels of our human sins and weaknesses. God's love seeks to win us to itself, that we might indeed become the full expression of that love to others.

In the end, our attitude should be one of amazement and adoration. God loves us and wants us to live as holy sons and daughters, sharing in the full inheritance of the Kingdom of Heaven. Our cosmic process may end at some point, but God's love will never end. That love promises that every ending will be turned into a new beginning, and that life will continue in ever greater joy and creative adventure, even when this earthly sojourn is over.

God is love, says the Bible, and with God there is no end. What we need to know now is how to appropriate and express that love.

---

[2] Ferre, Nels J. S. **The Christian Understanding of God.** New York: Harper & Brothers, 1951, 229.

[3] *Ibid.,* 204.

Chapter Three

The Myth Of The True Believer

George Orwell, best known for his 1948 novel of the future entitled **1984,** also wrote some essays which are even more incisive than his famed novel. In one of these essays he describes an experience from his boyhood:

A wasp was sucking jam on my plate, and I cut him in half. He paid no attention, merely went on with his meal, while a tiny stream of jam trickled out of his severed esophagus. Only when he tried to fly away did he grasp the dreadful thing that had happened to him.

Orwell went on to liken the condition of the severed wasp to that of modern man who had to have a form of religious belief cut away from him, but who for twenty years or more did not know what had happened.

Madeleine l'Engle reports this incident in one of her novels and suggests that Orwell's greedy wasp, unaware of its brokenness, is the Church. She says, "When Christian bodies war together as bitterly as we are doing, it would seem that some of us must be professing the antichrist. Once we recognize we're broken, we have a chance to mend, to become one."[4]

The warring and suspicion that goes on among Christian groups and individuals is scandalous. Much of it springs from a mythical notion that there is such a thing as the true believer, one who believes in the *full* gospel and who has all the right doctrines tucked firmly away in his head, as well as all the wrong ones turned decisively aside. Naturally, the true believer can tolerate no differences in viewpoints and makes no allowances for uncertainties or ambiguities in the matters of faith.

In many respects, the true believer has replaced the Pharisee of biblical times that Jesus denounced with such vehemence. Who is the true believer today, and how is he recognizable?

The true believer is a strict biblicist as well as a legalist. He insists that every word of the Bible is true, exactly as it was written (which really means as he interprets it). A lust for power hides behind his interpretations of the scriptures, for the true believer has a driving need to control and dominate. In many cases, he means to be honest, but he has repressed certain phases of his own seeing for so long, he can no longer view himself objectively. His demands for adherence to biblical authority make him deeply suspicious of any who reject matters as he sees them.

The true believer scorns the idea of unconditional love, because it is inconsistent with his view of God and totally outside his own experience. In fact, anything outside his experience is generally suspect. He has a secret pleasure in the fact that those in that category will someday be punished. While he may regret the imminent possibility of nuclear war, he may see it as the inevitable Armageddon, a time when evil will be destroyed.

The true believer cannot rally to any call for justice for people who are outside his own perimeters of faith, nor does he believe that the world can be changed or that it should be protected. The world is an evil place, at war with its Creator, and its destruction is both inevitable and desirable. He may scorn giving charitable help of any kind unless it will produce converts to his own way. He also has a sneaking suspicion that if people are poor or in some kind of trouble, they usually deserve it or have brought it upon themselves. He will support mission causes, but he does so more enthusiastically if there is at least one ocean between him and the field.

The true believer is more inclined to talk about Jesus than God, for Jesus has, in essence, become God for him. Instead of bowing before the mystery and marvel of Jesus, who became the Christ, he is inclined to trivialize Jesus by his own limited and dogmatic interpretations. He long ago shut the book on Jesus, nailing down his ideas and enshrining him in his own words and customs, so that he knows exactly where Jesus is and where he stands. He believes that no one can come to God except through Jesus, and he can quote one or two scripture passages to prove this. (He is, however, adept at ignoring any scriptures that call for an alteration of his intolerant and dogmatic viewpoints.) It goes without saying that the Jesus others must accept is the exact replica of the one he has accepted.

Although the true believer espouses a passion for saving souls, he generally holds contempt for the very ones he is supposedly trying to convert. He fails to see the inconsistencies in his behavior that ignores the mandate of the gospel to love. He camouflages his narrow-mindedness by claiming he has a devoted loyalty to Jesus, but in truth, the real Jesus Christ and the full power of the gospel are both emotionally and intellectually beyond him, for his conversion is only marginal. His personal insecurity and longing for power, joined with his historical heritage, have actually led him to evade the full demands of the gospel. He has built his faith on a fear of God. To him, God is a stern judge of grim vengeance and conditional love. There is a large portion of the true believer's life that he afraid to surrender to such a God. Consequently, he operates almost totally from a center of fear rather from a center of love.

The true believer is responsible for many of the extremist movements that have polarized the Christian body from within. These movements have encouraged separatism, and they stem from a paranoia that justifies excesses of militance and hostility. Since he always operates form the delusion of being right, he is quick to identify the enemy, the antichrist, and any other spirits of darkness, but he never sees any relationship between these entities and himself. His belief and his commitment are pathological, because they are governed by a deadly moral snobbism that thinks he and he alone has the truth.

Self-righteousness, contempt for others (at best a kind of supercilious pity), a spiritual arrogance blended with much pious ignorance—these are the marks of the true believer. Since everything outside himself and his own little system is scurrilous and depraved, what little love he can find in himself will usually be turned back to himself with the prayer, "I thank God I am not like others." Occasionally, when it is socially expedient, he may sound a loud cry in public, "God, be merciful to me, a sinner." But he is only going through the motions expected of him. Deep down he is satisfied that nothing is really wrong with him, because, after all, he is a true believer.

How do I know so much about the true believer? Because I have on more than one occasion found him living inside of me. At various points along my spiritual journey I have manifested nearly all his attitudes in one way or another. It was usually at the point my journey stopped and my quest ended. There is nowhere to go when you think you know it all. God has been patiently trying to excise these qualities from my life, as I have been willing to give free rein, but it has been a long battle, and it is not over yet.

Marks of the true believer live inherently in all believers. It really has nothing to do with being fundamentalist or liberal. It has to do with being intolerant or accepting. It has to do with being loving or unloving.

Whenever I meet someone in whom the true believer has nearly wrested full control (and institutional Christianity has many models), I struggle to offer them the same unconditional love that God has offered me in my own blindness. The struggle may be compounded by the fact that the true believer refuses to validate my position or give me the right to be who I am. It is difficult to love someone who will not grant you the freedom to be yourself and who repudiates the validity of something you hold dear. But it must be done if unconditional love is your goal.

The true believer has a counterpart. For lack of a better term, and to be inclusive in gender, I shall call her the poor believer.

The poor believer is one who can kneel at the feet of Jesus and confess, "I believe; help thou my unbelief." She knows that the ground upon which she walks in following Jesus is a ground alive with possibility yet fraught with mystery. No interpretation of Jesus has ever answered all her questions, so she has had to live out her questions in openness, wonder and gratitude. For her, Jesus is not a figure to be enshrined or particularized by definition. Rather, he is a figure who stands deep within history and deep within herself, a figure calling for her silent attention and her willing openness, a figure who entrusts her to bear his own quest.

The most constantly asked question about Jesus by the poor believer is the one often repeated in the gospels, "Who is this man?" As she considers the reality of his life, it is in a manner of profound reverence and even reticence. Yet her lack of definition about the exact nature of Jesus has not prevented her from following him obediently, living out her tensions courageously, and letting herself fall into both life and death with his gentle abandon, even with the willingness to let this life end without knowing the outcome. For the poor believer, Jesus is less a prisoner of her customs and words and more a questioner of her certainties. He and his way are less a sure word, less an easy foreverness, and more a mystery forever confounding her ease.

Yet it is precisely that tension that has inspired her to receive Jesus more fully into her life, allowing him to re-orient her values, re-define her hopes, and re-direct her ambitions. At the same time, she is under no illusion that others must find him in the same way she has done, nor does she think God has regard only for those who follow Jesus. God is too great to be mean and stingy about the path which people choose to reach him.

The poor believer recognizes the complexities of human nature, the hidden edges of motivations, the ambiguities of moral appraisals, and the blurred limits of virtue, because she has seen all these within herself. She has had a profound experience of God loving her despite her failures, and she feels compelled to do that for others. The poor believer does not feel she has to be indifferently cordial to all views and outlooks. She knows that limitless acceptance of differing views can only be afforded by those persons who are not very serious about anything. But she also knows that she has been called to love persons, no matter what they have done or are doing. She believes that this was somehow what Jesus did. He looked upon all manner of people, those broken with disease, afflicted with despair, angry with oppressions and injustices, in conflict with themselves and others, and still loved them. The only place where Jesus seemed to be harsh and con-demning was with the religionists (the true believers) who were unloving and uncaring for others.

When the poor believer prays, it is more an exercise of offering than of demanding, more an altar of receiving than a counter for ordering. She is overwhelmed by the mystery that through prayer she has access to the great God of the universe, yet she believes this to be true. So through prayer she attempts to keep open the link between her life and the Infinite Life, the link that will help her become what she was created to be. Her prayers then become a silent ingathering and a joyous and grateful selfgiving.

You will know the poor believer when you meet her. She is non-judgmental, accepting and tolerant. Above all, she is loving. If you were to comment openly on any of her attributes, she would be inclined to disbelieve you, for her goodness has grown in her so unconsciously that she is scarcely aware of it. Since she knows that truth is always larger than any version she might hold, she accepts the universe as her teacher and commits her life in trust to a process of eternal learning. The poor believer is both a disciple of inadequacy and a prophet of the future. She will lead the way for the coming generations, for she is offering to her children the will both to live and to love.

Each of us has a choice. We can be a true believer or a poor believer. Or we may choose to settle somewhere between, moving back and forth from one position to the next, until we are neither one nor the other, and hence not a believer at all.

Jesus said, "If your eye is single, your whole body will be full of light." It ought not to be too difficult for us to understand which choice he is asking us to make. Certainly we would be wise to heed his warning that not everyone who cries, "Lord, Lord," will enter the Kingdom of Heaven, while at the same time remembering he also said, "Blessed are the poor in spirit, for theirs is the kingdom of heaven."

---

[4] l'Engle, Madeleine. **A Severed Wasp**. New York: Farrar, Straus, Geroux, 1982.

Chapter Four

It All Begins With God

Unconditional love does not begin with us. It begins with God. We are incapable of reproducing or expressing it on our own. It is the highest gift of grace that God bestows upon his children when they sincerely open themselves to receive it. God's unconditional love comes at unsolicited times and in mysterious ways that defy our ability to explain or control. God gives unconditional love to us because God made us from divine essence. We are parts of God, and God is always striving to love us into our full and completed being.

A favorite author of mine from boyhood days was Zane Grey. Zane Grey gave up his profession of dentistry because of an overwhelming desire and conviction that he was meant to be a writer. He labored long and carefully over his first novel, submitted it to the publisher in New York City, and was then called by the publisher to come to the city for an interview. He was certain they were bringing him in to tell him they had accepted his book for publication.

Instead, the editor handed Grey his manuscript and said, "Mr. Grey, there is nothing in this to convince me you know how to write either fiction or narrative." The words so stunned the budding and hopeful author that he could scarcely see to walk out of the office.

Out on the street he stood, crushed beyond belief, his manuscript under his arm. He walked to a garbage can and was about to drop it in. but as he looked at it, he suddenly realized, "I created you. You are part of my life dream. If I deny you, I will deny myself."

He kept the manuscript, published it himself by drawing on all his savings, and continued to write. Ten years later, with the publication of **Light of the Western Stars,** he broke all sales records of any book to be published in 1914. By strict literary standards, Zane Grey was never a great writer. He was, however, a successful and popular author. Best of all, he got to do the thing he wanted to do. He fulfilled his life dream because he refused to deny it as a part of himself.

In the same way, God cannot deny us. God made us, and to deny us would be to deny Godself. We are each part of the great dream of God, and God loves us individually as a part of that dream. There is nothing we can do to earn this love, and there is really nothing we can do to end it. We can do many foolish things that cause us to lose awareness of that love, and if we had no early experience of being loved for the sake of ourselves, we may have grown up not knowing what love was all about. While this creates hurt and causes harm, neither is irreparable. Nor does this negate the fact that we are loved by God, not just for what we are but for what we can, in God's grace, become.

The Old Testament is strong on the notion that God judges us for our sins, but the New Testament pronounces a new truth: God forgives our sins. God has no need to judge us. Forgiveness becomes our judgment. Our own actions judge us by the way we keep or break the law of love. The New Testament affirms that God is kind, even to the ungrateful and the selfish (Luke 6:35). Fortunately this is so, or where would we be?

Most of us have probably believed at times that God has not always been good to us as we felt we deserved. And probably we have also concluded that God does not really punish sinners as swiftly or totally as we would wish. In fact, many of them seem to go scot-free. Sometimes the law of the land catches them and sends them to jail, but

God seems far less involved than we would like. As a result, we have pretty well left punishment up to law enforcement agencies, since we can't depend on God to do it. This has to occasion us with some bewilderment. Why doesn't God get busy and punish?

Traditional explanations from the church have said that punishment will come later. There is a hell where unrepentant sinners will get what is coming to them. The scales of justice will finally be balanced.

Actually, God neither rewards nor punishes. This refutes centuries of religious teachings, but I have come to believe strongly that this is so. There is a reward and punishment system that goes on in the world, and it is based on a law that Jesus taught, "As you sow, so shall you reap." Paul understood this law, for he wrote to the Christians in Galatia, "He that sows to his flesh shall of the flesh reap corruption, but he that sows to the Spirit shall of the Spirit reap life everlasting."

We may not think that the ancient law works as quickly or as effectively as it should, especially as we view those around who seemingly go unpunished for their wickedness. But the law is inflexible. What we give out, we will get back. It may not come back in the exact form it was sent out, but it does return. Deliver harm and evil to another, and you have delivered them to yourself.

Ignorance of this spiritual principle is what brings about most of our problems. The nature of evil is basically impersonal, and we need to stop blaming God for it. Once we can get over that hurdle, we will be a long way along the path to truth.

The basic secret of life is that there is only one life, and that life is God. This one life is unconditioned. It has no qualities of good or evil. It is a pure state of being, and it is neither good nor bad. Life, at its God essence, is a state of absolute being and perfection. It remains that until the dualistic belief of good and evil is accepted.

When a troubled person brings his problems to me, I have to be able to see that person as neither good nor bad if

I am going to help him. I must see him without my judgments imposed on him. Even "the true believer," that I described in the previous chapter, is not an evil person. He has accepted the dichotomy of good and evil into his belief system, which means that he views life as conditioned. Therefore, he cannot share in such a concept as unconditional love until he can drop his old beliefs. But at the essential level of his being, "the true believer" is a part of the essence of God, loved as much by God as "the poor believer."

There are not two powers in the universe. There is only one power, and that power is God. There is no such thing as bad power and good power, there is only unconditioned power. It is not mortal, it is not human, it cannot be analyzed, it cannot be described, it cannot be controlled, it cannot be purchased. The best protection we have is in knowing that this power is for us, all of us, because it is unconditioned. But we lose it when we try to condition it or when we try to turn it against one another.

Everything that springs from God is unconditioned. In God there is no such thing as disease and health, evil and good, old and young. In God, life is unconditioned, unfettered, and free. It knows neither good nor evil. It knows only the pure being and Spirit of God.

The gift of God to the world is love, and that love is not dependent upon how we behave or perform. It is ours when we choose to receive it. Jesus said to seek not after food, drink or clothing as priorities of life, but to seek first the Kingdom of God. In the Kingdom of God, love is the creative principle. Therefore, love must be the measure for the capacity of our good.

Love does not bring us success or happiness. Love goes far beyond such illusory experiences. Love brings us fulfillment, absolute and total. Love also brings a task to us, the task of expressing itself to others. But with the task it brings an understanding, a strength, and a wisdom that enables us to perform the task. We are not just told to love and then dumped out alongside the road as it were. When love is allowed to enter our lives, it brings whatever is necessary for its own fulfillment.

Unconditional love is the realization that God meets the needs of all persons, because God is the only one who truly knows those needs. Not even we know what we need. When we are ready for a spiritual truth, God will lead us to the particular teaching necessary for our unfoldment. We are each encouraged to follow the light that has been given to us by God. If we can allow this same freedom for others, we shall be living by the principle of unconditional love.

The Cheyenne Indians have a saying, "A man must do what he must. It is up to other men to understand and accept." This is part of the meaning of love without conditions. If what someone else does seems to be unacceptable or harmful, it is still our work to forgive and love. We must learn to honor the path another chooses, even though we do not choose that path for ourselves. If a person chooses to be a lawbreaker or to violate the rights and freedoms of another, it may be necessary to impose restrictions on his behavior. But those restrictions should be imposed in a spirit of love, not a spirit of vengeance.

When Jesus prayed from the cross, "Father, forgive them for they know not what they do," he did not mean that his murderers did not know what they were doing to him. They knew full well what they were doing to him. But they did not know what they were doing to themselves. That was his concern. The welfare of others is always the concern of unconditional love. God's love has only one concern: the well-being of God's creation, all of it.

Those who think that the world would benefit today by the nuclear incineration of the Soviet Union or the destruction of communist governments are sadly mistaken. Safety and security can never be found in the destruction of another. Safety and security can only be found in love. Love means care, care means protection, protection means security, and security means safety.

The history of the Christian church is sadly rent with attempts at inquisitions and reprisals of those who didn't fit the prescribed molds. Joan of Arc was condemned and burned at a stake, then declared a saint. Meister Eckhart, a German dominican monk who died in 1327, had problems with Roman authorities and many of his writings were condemned as heretical by Pope John XXII, yet today he is heralded as a great mystic. Pierre Teilhard de Chardin was once banned by the Roman church for his views but reinstated to good graces after his death. There have always been those individuals and groups within both Catholicism and Protestantism who have taken it upon themselves to discredit those who do not fit into their own patterns of thought. Such methods are essentially destructive and eventually futile. Truth cannot and will not be denied. Moreover, to attack the belief of another belies the true spirit of religion, unless, as in the case of Jesus' castigation of the Pharisees, that belief inspires contempt and mistreatment of others. It is only in our sense of separation from God that such things can happen, for God's will is unity and oneness. Yet in the church exist ardent believers who have failed to grasp what love means and who continue to suffer from and perpetuate the sin of separateness.

"What can separate us from the love of God?" asked the Apostle Paul when he was writing to the Romans. He mentioned some things that could not. But there is something that can separate us from the love of God: our own sense of separateness will do it. Our sense of having a life of our own that can begin and end with ourselves will do it. Our attempts to gain something at somebody's expense will do it. Our belief that destruction of another person, persons, or nations will benefit us, that will do it.

If we could learn the secret of unconditional love, which begins with God and is only found by a complete reliance on God, we would find a spiritual freedom in the outer realm that no one could take from us. From the law of love without conditions would come a total freedom from the desire or capacity to hurt others or to be hurt by them. Unconditional love reveals to us our divine inheritance as a holy son or daughter of God, and that same love will maintain and sustain our divinity under any and all circumstances.

Chapter Five

Forgiveness Is The Key

No ethic is stressed more in the Bible than forgiveness. In his eloquent and dynamic Sermon on the Mount, Jesus outlined the patterns for kingdom living. He returned to forgiveness several times as the imperative for the one who would be a disciple. Throughout his teachings, Jesus underscored the need for forgiveness and warned of the destructiveness of resentment.

Forgiveness is the key to sane, sensible living. It is also the key to the Kingdom of Heaven and the prerequisite of unconditional love. More than that, forgiveness is the initiatory act on our part that opens the way for God's forgiveness to come to us. The one condition that Jesus placed on God's forgiveness is our own willingness to forgive. A cursory reading of the New Testament should convince of this fact, yet many longtime students of the scriptures and sincere practitioners of the faith continue to balk at the level of forgiveness.

When wronged or hurt, our initial instinct is to strike back. It is a matter of patient and prolonged discipline to bring our unruly spirits under control, where we can with sincere authenticity turn the other cheek and be willing to go another mile.

Everything that happens to us in life is a lesson. Every experience offers us the opportunity for growth and good, if we can learn to forgive. Forgiveness is the key that releases the fulfillment of the scriptural promise, "All things work together for good to those who love God." We each hold that key in our hands, the key that opens the gates of Heaven and brings the unconditional love of God our Heavenly Father-Mother down to earth at last. If we take the first little step, which is to say, "I will forgive," God will take the final steps and bring our forgiveness to completion.

I once heard Walter Brueggemann, Bible scholar and professor, say that forgiveness means two things: (1) the past is past, we yield it in favor of hope; (2) we are willing for a genuine redistribution of power. Let us examine forgiveness under these two headings.

We Yield The Past In Favor Of Hope

All of us, without very much effort, can look back in our lives and find places where we have been hurt. In some cases that hurt may be so deep and raw that we have covered it up by attempting to block it from our conscious memories. Nevertheless, it is still there. Like a festering cancer that silently does its deadly work while we are unaware, that place of hurt and pain continues to inflict its poison into our system. It influences the ways we behave and react to others and eventually wrecks our health.

Many of these places of hurt are found in the confusing and sometimes hopeless tangle of family relationships. Where love is imbalanced or impoverished, the family, our greatest seedbed of promise, becomes the source of lifelong trouble and revenge. Wherever parents direct arbitrary love or harsh treatment and stern force against their children, the children suffer and often perpetuate those same patterns to their children when they become parents. We know from experience that abused children become abusive parents, if the cycle is not somehow broken.

Betrayals and hurts in the family are not easily overcome. They have lingering power. But that cycle of pain must be broken if we are to move on whole and free. Sooner or later we must put the past behind us by learning to forgive those who have wronged or hurt us. Only in this way can we come out from our exile and alienation and free those who are restricted and in bondage to our resentments.

Forgiveness is the single crucial sign of the Christian. It is the one thing that makes a Christian different from all others. It is not because a Christian is saved or favored or enlightened that a Christian is different. It is because a Christian forgives. We are called upon to love our enemies, to bless those who persecute us, to forgive those who wrong us, to be reconciled to those who hurt us. As long as we seek to justify our resentments and validate our hurts, we will get nowhere. As soon as we enter into the argument that says, "But it wasn't my fault," then we are hopelessly mired. It has nothing to do with whose fault it is. Forgiveness has to do with letting go of the past and yielding it in favor of a future of hope and freedom.

Our family relationships may never be all we would like them to be. We may not be able to bring those that have hurt us into line with our own forgiving intentions. We may have to accept the fact that there might never be real closeness or sincere compatibility with everyone we would like, even members of our own family. But this must not hold us back from forgiving. We forgive because we know it is the only way we can be free and the only way we can offer the possibility of freedom to others.

We Are Willing For
A Genuine Redistribution Of Power

Forgiveness is not just a spiritual notion, any more than love is. Forgiveness is a decisive act that says to another:

"I will give something for you. I will stop seeing you as an enemy or as an object of my anger and revenge. I will share myself with you, and I will give you the only gift that I want for myself—forgiveness. I will not view you as less than whole or as unworthy in any way. I want the best for you, and I will now remove the resentment and anger I have built around you, in order that you will not be bound in any way by me from your own quest for understanding and truth."

Forgiveness must be a visible demonstration that we are willing to share ourselves, our power, and even our possessions, if need be. I am well aware that this is not the way of the world, and that anyone who takes this teaching literally will immediately be branded as foolish if not downright "crazy." But it is the way of love, and ultimately it is the way to freedom and victory. History carries many sad tales where unforgiveness, deteriorating into vengeance and greed, has wrought severe suffering on the world.

Even as I write this, I am mindful of the conflicts that rage so bitterly in our world in such places as Northern Ireland, Palestine, South Africa, and in several countries in South America. It is hard to believe that any dream of liberation and redistribution of power can ever be accomplished in these places where the future seems only a replay of the past.

But lift your eyes above the problems for a moment and remember that the Bible affirms that God has a purpose for this world which is finally sovereign. That purpose may be held temporarily in abeyance because of the dark side of human action and planning, but it will come through. It will work through human action if possible, and it will even work against human action, if necessary, for its final realization. The power of God's dream for this world as a world where all people live in peace and harmony with each other and all creation will not be altered or destroyed. It may be delayed, but it will come about. This is the inexorable and persistent message of the Bible. This God-dream finds its focus in Jesus' preaching of the Kingdom of Heaven, a Kingdom both realized and yet to come.

Most of us do not have the opportunity to influence the course of world history by our actions. We are not in places of prominence or importance where we can make decisions that affect the lives of thousands or even hundreds. And yet in one sense each of us is in such a place.

One small act of forgiveness does something beneficial and ennobling for the entire human race. It sends forth a vibratory current into the atmosphere that carries its own profound and revitalizing effect. The thoughts we think affect our destiny and the destiny of others. We literally dwell in a sea of thoughts and ideas. Many of these are negative and destructive. A loving thought, a genuine act of forgiveness, released into the atmosphere, is an antidote to the negativisms that surround us. Love and forgiveness purify the environment in which we live.

What I am saying may sound terribly simplistic and naive, but I assure you it has its roots in any study being made today of the rational systematization of human energy. If love is the highest form of human energy, and if human energies radiate into the cosmic mass to set in motion what Pierre Teilhard de Chardin called the "noosphere" (the idea of a new thinking layer being formed on the earth, which is alternately called a new skin of the earth's soul), then it follows that love is the highest form of transformational energy that can be released. It literally changes our environment.

Love impregnates the universe like an oil that will revive its colors, says Teilhard, and can melt the multitude of our perceptions and emotions in a single impression. He points out that two thousand years ago when the words, "Love one another," were pronounced, we thought they meant, "Love one another in order to be perfect." But today, as our perceptions and understandings have increased, we have come to understand their meaning as "Love one another or you perish."[5]

Our survival depends upon love. All attempts at human collectivizations are ending up, contrary to our hopes and predictions, in a lowering and an enslavement of human consciousness. Love is the only possibility of unification. It is the only thing capable of bringing humans together in a way that will complete and fulfill them, for love alone joins us to what is deepest in ourselves and in each other.

But how far must this love extend? How universal must our forgiveness be? When Peter asked this question of Jesus, he suggested in a sly manner that perhaps seven times was an acceptable limit. Jesus, with droll wit but deadly seriousness, said seventy times seven was even better. His meaning was clear. There can be no limits.

Opponents of this seemingly impossible demand say that human capacity to love and forgive is of necessity confined to a very few. It is impossible for the human heart to go beyond a limited radius, so to love all and forgive everyone is a contradictory, false gesture, which only leads in the end to loving and forgiving no one.

But as Teilhard says, "If, as you claim, a universal love is impossible, how can we account for that irresistible instinct in our hearts which leads us towards unity whenever and in whatever direction our passions are stirred?"[6]

There are moments when we are seized by compassion for the *All*, when we are literally in love with everyone and everything. These moments often come to us when confronted by a great beauty in nature, music, or some other form of creativity, but they are not confined to these. I have personally had occasions when I was speaking to a huge roomful of people, many whom I did not know, and felt seized by a deep, tremendous love for them, a love which was so overpowering it made me want to weep. What was it? It was an awareness of a Great Presence in our midst, revealing a deep accord between all the realities that had come together seeking each other. It was the transcendant empowerment of Unconditional Love. A universal love and forgiveness may indeed be psychologically impossible, but not spiritually. It is the only complete and final way in which we are able to love. It is a gift of grace that no one can account for, except the One who gives it.

If universal love is possible, and if it is most easily

apprehended in the religious experience, how can we explain the mounting repulsion and hatred, the spirit of meanness and suspicion, that seems to be sweeping through the church at this moment? Just this. There are many significant new modes of thought breaking in on the human scene just now, especially on the spiritual level. The old does not easily give itself up to the new. The spiritual explorer who dares introduce such a concept as universal love and forgiveness is a threat to those whose love is limited and conditioned. The explorer is regarded as a pressing danger, for the new light will unveil the ignorance of the past. The enthusiasm and understanding of the explorer will lay bare the lack of trust, the self-centeredness, and the duality of the one who no longer quests. The search is over for the one who feels he has found everything. No more explorations are allowed.

This is the true believer syndrome again, rising up to assert control. Whenever one becomes harsh and unforgiving, as in the case of Christians who war with other Christians or religious groups, it is usually a projection of one's fears and unresolved guilts. There is nothing to do when this happens but to love and forgive the one who is fearful and wait for the day when the love he has been trying to kill shall come to birth in his own heart.

What could you want forgiveness cannot give?
Do you want peace? Forgiveness offers it.
Do you want happiness, a quiet mind,
A certainty of purpose, and a sense
Of worth and beauty that transcends the world?
Do you want care and safety, and the warmth
Of sure protection always? Do you want
A quietness that cannot be disturbed,
A gentleness that never can be hurt,
A deep, abiding comfort, and a rest
So perfect it can never be upset?
Here is your answer! Would you stand outside
While all of heaven waits for you within?
Forgive and be forgiven. As you give

You will receive. There is no plan but this
For the salvation of the Son of God.[7]

[5] Teilhard de Chardin, Pierre. *loc. cit.*, 128-130, 144-155.

[6] Teilhard de Chardin, Pierre. **The Phenomenon of Man**, Trans. Bernard Wall. New York: Harper & Row, 1959, 266.

[7] **Choose Once Again. Selections from "A Course in Miracles."** Eds. Julius J. Finegold and William N. Thetford. Millbrae, California: Celestial Arts, 1981, 85.

Chapter Six

Prayer Is The Door

What is notably absent in most discussions of love is the mention of prayer. That is unfortunate for two reasons. First, prayer, when rightly understood and rightly used, is the highest form of love we can express. Second, prayer at its pinnacle is the door whereby the unconditional love of God can enter into our lives to purify our own love and transform our every enterprise and effort.

Prayer has a twofold objective. It gives us an opportunity to talk to God, and it gives God an opportunity to talk to us. The latter is much more important that the former. While talking *to* God may occasion us with psychological satisfaction, it offers only minimum advancement to our spiritual growth and understanding. Letting God talk to us is infinitely more valuable.

Just as there are many kinds of love, there are many kinds of prayer. The prayer I propose to talk about here is the contemplative prayer of self-giving whereby one offers oneself to God for the awakening of the holy, mystical consciousness that is within all of us but rarely discovered.

Howard Thurman, the great American mystic, defined religious experience as "the conscious and direct exposure of the individual to God."[8] This exposure is necessary in order for truth to be experienced. Truth is more than an idea or a belief; it is Reality itself. An individual must encounter it with the whole self, body, mind and spirit. There is nothing that is not involved.

The most important activity of the religious experience for the individual is prayer. But whereas prayer in many religions is based on the conviction that God is a reality which exists independently of all subjective experience, it is my conviction that God is most clearly discovered in one's inner experience. Here the contact is direct and immediate, and God is perceived as the only Reality.

The most important activity of God is loving. God's love gives definition to God's nature and indicates how that nature acts upon and cares for the individual and the community. God can only be known through love, and the fullest meaning of love is to be found in the inner religious experience. Thurman explains that "in the religious experience, the individual finds fulfilled what he has glimpsed in his other expressions of love: namely, that in the presence of God he becomes aware of being dealt with totally."[9]

Thurman's mysticism, which has had a profound influence on my own, holds that religious experience affirms rather than negates the world. Encounter with God gives a perspective on how one is to be committed to society and how to recognize and deal with evil. As new moral-ethical insights emerge, the individual is obligated to become a part of transforming the world.

The contemplative life also develops a sense of universality. It does not take us long in the silence to realize that God is a Spirit within our own being and fully available to us. If available to us, then that Spirit is also available to anyone of any faith or no faith. All that is needed is a hunger for God and a recognition that God is. God will do the rest, leading us gradually to a total love for everyone and everything.

That is why the contemplative or inner life can lead the way to world peace. It creates a love affair with the universe. It does not build fences around God and it does not lay down dogmatic rules. Rather, it recognizes God as the only life there is, the Universal Life. To destroy any part of that life is to destroy a part of God. This recognition comes to us very early when silent prayer is practiced. There is only one God, belonging to everyone; hence, all men and women belong to God and are brothers and sisters. The imperative that follows then is to treat each other as members of the same family, a united household.

To do this wipes out two of the most important causes of war: religious controversies and economic rivalries. When we can learn to love one another as God loves us, we have set a pattern for individual and world harmony. A single individual, realizing within himself or herself that God is a Universal Spirit through whom we are all related to one another, can begin to free the world from its balance of fear.

This is not a new concept. Wiser men and women than I have said this for centuries. It is just that we cannot seem to get it into our consciousness deeply enough to live by it. We have come to rely too strongly on outer forms of power—mental, material, or some other kind. But in the inner life all power has to be released. We have to lay down our arms and come to God as open and as empty as possible. We do not come to God only to be comforted in our hurts and healed of our sufferings. We do not come to God for superior wisdom and strength. All that will happen, but it will not happen until we can first appear before God empty-handed and open-hearted and want God for God's sake rather than for any gifts God may give. We can pray to God to end wars until we are blue in the face, but this will not happen. The only way wars will end is for armies to run out of ammunition and agree to lay down their arms. So when we come to God, we must make sure that we have surrendered every kind of power on which we have been leaning except the one Power, God, besides which there is no other power.

No one knows exactly where contemplative prayer or meditation first began. It was practiced in the Eastern world long before it ever reached the West. In our Judeo-Christian tradition, it was probably a Moses or a David who was a traveler on the deserts or in the mountains. He had a lot of time to observe the heavens and note the mysteries of nature. He was conscious of the marvelous fecundity of his flocks and fields. At some point, after contemplating these wonders for a period of time, a sense of inner peace, mingled with an ecstatic kind of exhilaration must have entered into his consciousness, and he experienced a great infilling of love and an upsurging of peace. The longer he continued with this experience, the greater became his sense of oneness with God and with everything.

At precisely such a moment, God laid the mantle on the shoulders of Moses to lead his people out of bondage and slavery. He placed in the heart of David the vision of leaving his flocks and becoming a great ruler of his people. Yet if either Moses or David had come to God with such a desire or request, seeking personal greatness or power, nothing would have happened. It is precisely when we are "lost in wonder, love and praise" emptied of self-seeking, that the miracles come, followed by the commission to translate the miracles into loving service. Through an inner communion with Something greater than ourselves, we discover we are never alone and that life does have meaning and purpose. We also discover that we are loved with a love greater than the universe, a love which is waiting to be recognized so it may be bestowed, a love from which we can draw for wisdom, guidance, healing and strength.

Contemplative prayer helps us become what Joel Goldsmith, the internationally known spiritual leader, has termed a beholder. [10] We are invited to step off the stage of life for a time and watch life unfold before our eyes. We see ourselves objectively and watch the other players on the stage with us going through their headaches, heartaches and grief. But like watching a movie whose ending has already been revealed to us, we know that everything will ultimately turn out well. There is a happy ending, one that we can help bring about by regularly taking time to step aside and looking at life as God sees it. This is what contemplative prayer will do for us: it will help us become beholders of life, that we might return to the world as wiser and more compassionate participants.

Contemplative prayer also leads us into the realization that God has a divine plan for the lives of each of us, a plan that is destined to bring us to our highest attainment and greatest good. It is at this level that the writings of Glenn Clark have been immensely helpful to me. He was a college professor and the founder of Camps Farthest Out. He was also a veteran explorer of the inner life who has shared his insights in a number of books. When I first read **The Divine Plan,** a little pamphlet by Glenn Clark, it was like a seed had been planted in my heart which has been steadily growing ever since. The belief that God has a plan for me, and that as I yield myself to God that plan expresses itself more perfectly through me, helped me realize that my essence does not consist in just being myself. Rather, my essence comes in yielding myself to God and letting the divinity that is in me manifest through me to the universe. My individual plan then becomes part of God's larger plan for the good of all. It is not something separate for me alone.

Anxiety, uncertainty, fear, jealousy, anger—these are not part of the Divine Plan for any of us. Contemplative prayer helps remove these enemies from us and gives us a vision of what is ours to have and to do. We can indeed possess all things, but only in God. In possessing God we possess everything, because God is the creator and owner of all things. Yet we can never fully possess God. The best we can hope to do is to make more room in our lives for God to possess us.

At our home in Seattle we have a large open patio between the front of the house and the garage. The roof on this patio is glass. While it is a delightful passageway for us, it occasionally becomes a trap for flying insects and birds. They fly into the patio and then strike against the skylights, trying in desperate futility to get out. Before their very eyes they can see a great sea of light, and yet they are not able to escape their prison. Usually birds will eventually determine that their freedom is found not by flying upward, but by flying out through either side. But for some reason bees and other flying insects cannot figure this out. They buzz angrily and helplessly against the glass until finally they drop to the floor, exhausted and dying.

Often I see humans going through the same futile exercises, yearning for the light and the freedom, but colliding against the obstacles that offer a concrete resistance and thus inhibiting their movement to God. They see the promise of light but fail to reach it.

Not until we forget our fascination with the light and turn back toward the darkness shall we find the exit into freedom and openness, into God. We must face courageously and honestly the dark side of ourselves, the shadowy deceptions and willful recalcitrance that live in all of us, before we can be free to begin our exploration of the allness of God. Nor can we ignore the darkness of the world by turning our backs upon such things as hunger, poverty and discrimination, and pretending that these things do not exist. We must gather these into our consciousness and then turn to God for the healing, the forgiving, and the transmuting that is needed.

Prayer must undergird every step of our quest for love. Only God has full access to our interiority. Only God has the key to our being. Prayer, which is a self-offering, a yielding up of the totality of one's being to the One who created us in love, brings us into the fullness of ourselves and into loving communion with all that God has created.

Each of us bears the mark of divinity. Ernesto Cardenal, a Latin American theologian, says we are all fingerprints of God. Prayer reveals the divinity that is part of our true nature and sets us free to be agents of unconditional love and healers of the great cosmic anguish.

The basic and primary sin of humankind is to believe that we know better than God what is good for us. We live in exile as long as we continue with such thinking. Our love becomes perverted into a kind of self-love that turns in on itself and does not differ actually from the hatred of others. True love is the self-giving of one person to another and the self-giving of a person to God. In this love comes our true freedom.

God in Christ has given Godself to us. As we receive that gift, our love is purified, and we become part of the redemptive process that has been seeking through the centuries to return this world to its divine image.

8   Thurman, Howard. **The Creative Encounter.** New York: Harper & Brothers, 1954, 20.

9   Thurman, Howard. **The Growing Edge.** New York: Harper & Row, 1956, 27.

10 Goldsmith, Joel. **The World Is New.** New York: Harper & Brothers, 1962, 47-59.

Chapter Seven

What To Do
When Bad Times Come

Elaine lived a desperate, wracked life. She drifted from one counselor and spiritual teacher to another, seeking surcease from her grief and balm for her bitterness. She had dwelt so long with her pain that it had become the reason for her existence. She clutched it to herself like a garment, examining it frequently and reviewing its condition so often that it soon became apparent to the observer that she had no wish to let it go. If she did, she would have to invent a new reason for living.

What had happened to Elaine to produce such crippling results? Some years ago she had lost her only child, a handsome, talented thirteen-year-old boy. On a dark, rainy night a driver of an automobile, failing to see the lad on his bicycle, had struck and killed him. Elaine had no one else. Abandoned some years earlier by her husband, the father of the child, she had since lived solely for the boy. With him gone, she had only the bitter memories of his death.

Although she said she wanted to be free from her grief, it was apparent that she did not mean it. Either she could not or would not free herself from the anguished bonds of sorrow that had intermingled with the strangling resentment she carried against the driver who had taken her son's life. On each anniversary of his death, she went deeply into the original grief and emerged more twisted, more unforgiving, more resentful. There was not even a balm to be found in religion, for she was unable to get beyond the despairing question, "Why did God allow this to happen?" Her health was breaking, both mentally and physically. Her friends were drifting away, put off by her inordinate self-pity. The net was closing ever more tightly around her.

Finally one counselor had the courage to confront Elaine honestly and almost brutally with the fact that her torture and suffering were basically self-inflicted and self-defeating. No one was punishing her. God had not caused the boy's death, nor had the driver of the car been malicious in his intent. Who, then, was responsible? Was it Elaine?

"You lead me to believe you were the perpetrator of your own son's death," said the counselor. "By some devious twist of logic you have assumed responsibility. Had you not given him the bicycle, had you not allowed him out of the house, had you been more restrictive and less indulgent, it would not have happened."

His remarks cut and offended her deeply, and Elaine protested angrily that she had loved the boy more than life itself, that she had wanted only the best for him and would never have hurt him for any reason.

"But you persist in acting as though you were to blame," said the counselor. For the first time, someone was offering more to Elaine than sympathy. By a technique similar to shock therapy, he helped her see how faulty her reasoning, how circular her rationalization, how destructive her attitude. Gradually she was led to understand that the only saving route open to her was forgiveness, acceptance and love.

Elaine was finally able to become a "beholder." In the pain of the confrontation with the counselor, she saw through new eyes and realized there might never be an answer to her why, but if she wanted to have a life beyond her present existence of recrimination and bitterness, she would have to construct it. Through additional therapy sessions and strong prayer support, she learned to forgive the driver of the car, to forgive herself, and, finally, to accept her son's death in peace.

Elaine is a real person, but she is a symbol that is almost universal. "Elainism" is an affliction that besets many at times. It is the tendency we all have to take the bad things of life, whenever they come, and internalize them to the point of futility. Suffering is universal and bad times are indiscriminate. They come to everyone at one time or another. Since we cannot avoid them, what can we do about them?

Our first strategy should be to abandon the why and move to the how. How we meet bad times is more important than trying to decide why they come. But our immature minds refuse this logic. We require an explanation of some sort before we are willing to tackle the solution. Various reasons, therefore, have been advanced as to why people suffer. Here are some traditional explanations:

1. *God gives us what we deserve; our misdeeds and sins cause our misfortunes.* This is a neat package, but it offers no help when opened. It induces greater guilt and blame, making people hate God as well as themselves. Obviously a God of unconditional love would not treat his children this way. Jesus was adamant that our Heavenly Father-Mother God gives better gifts to us than even the best earthly parents give to their children.

2. *There is a devil in the universe who slips up on our blind side and lets us have it.* Again, this is a neat, disposable method and attractive to many, because it offers a scapegoat. It does, however, create a theological problem of a good god and a bad god with humanity caught between. If God is unconditional love, and if unconditional love is unconditioned power, then there is really only one Power, God. There may be an evil force in the universe, the collective unconscious of all human evil,

but that force is basically impersonal, and it is a force that is dissipated before a God of unconditional love.

3. *We need suffering. It is a test that will ennoble, expand, educate and eradicate evil from our lives. Therefore, God gives bad times to us because they will help us grow.* Again, this proposition makes God sadistic. We need not deny that suffering can have an ennobling dimension and a purifying purpose. But why must we persist in accusing God of causing it?

4. *God has a pattern, and we are only seeing part of it. It is like looking at a tapestry from the wrong side; every twist and knot has a place in the grand design, but we are not able to see it yet. Someday we will see the tapestry of life from the right side and will understand.* I can see limited value in this viewpoint, as long as we don't try to apply it too widely, and as long as we don't make God responsible for every thread in the pattern. To say of the holocaust that God had a pattern and that Hitler and Nazi Germany were instruments in its production is not only sheer stupidity but utterly abhorrent. The only good that can emerge from the holocaust is the determination that something like that shall never happen again. It is true we do not see the whole pattern and the final outcome, but it is also true that human ignorance and sin have altered the original design of God's creation. We humans often create our own suffering, and we are often responsible for causing suffering to those who are innocent.

I could go on and list more traditional answers, but we must come to see that none of these answers is conclusive or satisfactory. There is something we are missing or perhaps incapable of finding just now. The why of bad times may continue to elude us, even though we continue to make our assessments of blame. The disturbing question of why we live in a universe where suffering and pain seem so rampant and at times uncontrolled and indiscriminate may only be answered in the future when we have advanced spiritually and are wiser than we are at the moment. For now, we must be honest and say that we do not always know why bad times come.

However, there are some things we do know with certainty. Suffering and bad times are not a total waste. Infinite good can emerge from even the worst scenario. Suffering does indeed expand character. It releases courage. This is not to say that suffering produces courage. Rather, it reveals and calls forth the courage that is already there. God does not need evil in order to produce good, any more than we need suffering to make courage. But out of the dark times emerges the light, and the light coming from the darkness is infinitely greater and more powerful than any we might otherwise experience. The dark side of nature seems to be an indispensable part of this earthly sojourn, and to deny that side is to deny part of our growth.

Suffering also releases compassion. People who have suffered deeply have a compassion and a wisdom unmatched and often unsung. Once they pass beyond the hurdle of "Why me?" and out of the valley of self-pity and guilt, they usually become giants of compassion, with the ability to minister to other sufferers in uncannily effective ways.

Peg and Bill are friends of mine who have a son who, in his late teens, was diagnosed as having paranoid schizophrenia. Schizophrenia is a disease that we are just beginning to understand, although there is much that we do not yet know, including effective treatment. It is characterized by the presence of conflicting emotions, irrational impulses and bizarre ideas. It can strike anytime, yet most often makes its appearance when the victim is in his or her late teens. Rob, the son of Peg and Bill, was a handsome 6' 2" winner of gold medals in swimming and cross-country, a governor's scholar, musician, artist, and whiz mathematician. Suddenly, at age nineteen, he thought he was the reincarnation of the philosopher Nietzsche. Having been born in Saudi Arabia when his parents were there with an oil company, Rob, with his new misperception of the world, recalled his early Sunday school stories of the prophets, and concluded that he, too, by reason of birthplace, must have a mission to save the world. The Rob whom Peg and Bill had known and loved for nineteen years disintegrated into a troubled and confused stranger.

The diagnosis of paranoid schizophrenia was totally unacceptable to Peg and Bill at first. There was nothing like this in their families. Surely someone had given him LSD or some potent mind-altering drug. They were unavoidably filled with "Elainism" and posed the classical question, "How could God do this to us?" They had tried to honor God in every way they could.

After their initial reactions had run their course, they set to work to understand what had happened and how to work with it. They discovered that schizophrenia is a mental illness that affects 1% of the general population. It may be caused by a biochemical imbalance in the brain, information we have only recently acquired. The factors of individual biochemistry, environment, heredity, nutrition and stress all play a role (to what degree is yet unknown) to precipitate this devastating illness. It is marked by delusional thinking, hallucinations, fear of others, withdrawal, and an almost total breakdown of the ego. Its final tragic result can be total disintegration of the personality.

Within the next four years Rob was seen by twenty-three different psychiatrists, survived three suicide attempts, four hospitalizations, participated in a "hemodialysis-for-schizophrenia" project (which didn't work), had brain scans, innumerable tests, and hundreds of hours of talk therapy. Peg and Bill wondered what God wanted them to do with this nightmare.

They became aware of the unutterable loneliness of

their situation and their need for support. Realizing there must be others like themselves, they helped form a support group for parents and relatives of mentally ill people in their area. It grew so large and effective that they tied in with state and national organizations for the mentally ill, whose membership is in the thousands and covers the entire country. They combined their forces to bring about the necessary changes in legislation so badly needed in the field of mental health treatment and research.

Rob became better. His mind became clear and his thinking straight. However, the nature of the illness is cyclical, and after a period of health, he again attempted suicide by an overdose. Peg and Bill continued to stand by him as they worked to help others in similar straits. Bill accepted a position on the Board of Directors for the California Alliance for the Mentally Ill (CAMI), where he now spends several days a week in Sacramento working on legislation for the mentally ill. His time for this is all voluntary. Peg went back to school to complete her degree, and at the present she is considering further training to be qualified for one of the helping professions. They are people who have come through a dark nightmare of torture, a nightmare that is not yet over, and are emerging from it stronger people with a greater sense of calling to serve the world. In a recent letter to me Peg wrote, "Gone are the days of impatience. I wait for God's plan to unfold and reveal itself. My lamp of good hope burns brightly."

Peg and Bill's story is almost a direct parallel with that of Wilton and Lloyd, members of my present church. They are presently suffering through a nearly identical situation with their son Craig. Like Peg and Bill, they have learned to turn their suffering into service and to bring attention to a problem that has long been ignored and misunderstood. Lloyd serves on the King County Mental Health Board, and together with Wilton is translating despair into compassionate hope.

The Bills and Pegs, the Lloyds and Wiltons, teach us

much about what to do when dark days come. It isn't what happens to us that matters; it's how we deal with what happens. There is an old proverb that says, *Do what you can and endure what you must.* It is good advice for the dark times.

Rabbi Harold S. Kushner created some stir among religious folks when he suggested in his best seller, **When Bad Things Happen to Good People,** that God can't do everything; yet Kushner is right. There are certain situations God cannot reverse, certain conditions God cannot (or will not) change. For God to intervene and rescue us from our problems might deprive us of valuable opportunities for spiritual growth and service, something that would only be ours by working through the problem. God has promised never to abandon us and to give us unfailing strength and undying love. The question before us then, when something bad happens, need not be, "How can I get out of this?" but rather, "How can I win some good from this?" That is the kind of question God delights in helping us answer.

Let me suggest a few simple rules that might help us escape the tensions and destructiveness of the bad times. No such list can ever be complete in and of itself, but perhaps it can be a start in reclaiming the light that the darkness has temporarily obliterated.

1. *Be willing to have the bad times end and willing to accept any help that will bring this about.* Your own willingness to emerge is crucial. Accept the bad times, but don't accept them as permanent. And don't be afraid to reach out for help and support.

2. *Look beyond yourself.* Don't get so absorbed in your problem that you have no interest in or devotion to anything beyond yourself. Self-pity compounds any problem. There is a paradoxical truth that in losing life to something beyond ourselves we gain life. Get busy serving others, and don't be hesitant to look beyond yourself to God. God has

been waiting for just such a moment and will be there to give you comfort and courage.

3. *Strive for a perspective on what is important and what is not.* We often make a great fuss over trivial matters. Ask yourself, "Why does this matter so much to me? How is it important to the wider plan of life?" It may be that the dark days can be brightened, simply by a sharpening of perspective.

4. *Change the things you can and accept the things you cannot change.* Do it without inner rebellion. Some things are unalterable or inevitable—death, losses, certain kinds of illness, separations, etc. But some things can be changed. Search for the wisdom to know the difference between the things you can change and the things you must accept.

5. *Keep faith in the fact that life has meaning.* Life is difficult, and life may not always seem to be fair. But ultimately life has meaning. Refuse to give in. Hold to the truth, "This too shall pass."

6. *Don't be too brave about it.* That isn't any good in the long run. It is our weakness and our need of God that God loves best. Our sufferings give God the chance to begin with us all over again, and in our weakness God's strength is made perfect.

7. *Above all, look to the way of unconditional love as your highest answer.* Ask yourself, "How can I release love into this situation so that healing may begin?" Pray always to be filled with love and forgiveness so that you harbor no resentment against anyone or anything. Be at peace with the knowledge that God is ever at work on your behalf and will never abandon you. And remember that love is the great miracle worker that makes all things work together for good.

In a time of physical suffering in my own life, which was also accompanied by some mental stress, I had the opportunity to discover something that strengthened my ability to cope. It was a cold, rainy day, and I wanted a fire in the fireplace. There was no wood in the house, so I went out into the storm and gathered several wet, dirty pieces of wood into my arms and carried them into the house where they could dry. As I embraced those sticky logs and felt them leaving their soil and pitch on me, it suddenly became clear that this is how I must deal with my time of darkness. I must embrace my pain and carry it until I come to the place where I can lay it down. That will be the place where the pain can be surrendered and transmuted into a higher energy. I do that in the same way I carry the logs of wood to the fire, unpleasant though that might be. But unless I do that, there is no opportunity for the wood to be burned and changed into new energies of warmth and light. So we must embrace our pain and journey with it until we reach the place where we can let it go.

We have become a people afraid of darkness and suffering. Otto Rank and Ernest Becker are two thinkers who feel that our Western culture has a fear and denial of death, and that we have been in flight from all forms of darkness for generations. We are unwilling to dive into the depths of our beings and to acknowledge what we might find there. We are unwilling to think that we may have to endure even so much as one hour of pain. Becker, Rank, Jung and such religious thinkers as Matthew Fox, Henri Nouwen, and Thomas Merton are among those who encourage us to befriend the darkness, to embrace the pain, and to realize that it is in the darkness that the new life always begins.

Matthew Fox, a Dominican scholar and innovative educator, in his book, **Original Blessing** (which I will refer to in a later chapter), tells us that life is a series of birthings, and that the birthing process is a place of darkness and struggle, as well as a place of freedom and light. If we do not embrace the darkness, we shall never achieve the light.[11]

Even now, new ideas and new awarenesses are

struggling to be born in the consciousness of all of us. We may be facing circumstances that are imprisoning us and forcing us to let go of our light-of-day plans. But we can let the darkness and the pain become the fuel for our journey into the light.

This was the way of Jesus Christ. He did not allow the cross to use him; he used it. He took hold of the situation and reacted positively and creatively. He embraced the darkness of the cross and offered it to God, and on that day the cross was changed from a symbol of punishment into a symbol of hope and redemption for the world.

Paul said that "in everything God works for good with those who love him" (Romans 8:28). God is not responsible for everything, but God will work with us to rescue the good that lies dormant in everything. In every circumstance and situation, no matter how dark, the ultimate triumph of God awaits. By making our life journey one that accepts both the darkness and the light, we become whole, we become holy.

No matter how much we talk about the value of giving, the brutal fact is that none of us has anything to give anyone. We are all creatures of need. The only thing we really know how to do is receive. We came into the world with open hands, and it is how we must leave it. We can give nothing. We can only receive. But it is in the receiving we grow and mature. There is nothing then to do when dark days come but to lift up our emptiness to God and receive the gifts of love that God is always waiting to give. All suffering is potentially redemptive, and when our cup is filled to overflowing, it will go forth to bless the entire world.

---

[11] Fox, Matthew. **Original Blessing.** Santa Fe, New Mexico: Bear & Company, Inc., 134-139.

Chapter Eight

Where Are You In Your Family?

The family is the place where we first learn to love. In ideal family relationships we have our first encounter with the highest and most desirable of loves—love without conditions. Our families exert more influence on us than any other institution, organization, or event. Even after we grow up, move away, and start building our own families, that influence persists and affects the structures of our new family units. Our basic personality is imprinted by what takes place in the family. Our basic value system is set in place largely by the family. How parents interact with each other and with each child as it enters the family determines to a large degree what shall be the final destiny of the child.

Some significant studies have been conducted on birth order. It is now generally believed that where you are in your family helps determine to a large degree why you are as you are. I have yet to come across a birth order study that is dogmatic in saying that all first-born children are one way, all second-born another way, and all last-born a still different way. There are tendencies and general characteristics that often apply, but every family is different in the dynamic of its relationship. So at the outset of this chapter, it is important to underscore that birth order is not a final determinant. But it can be an indication of why you are the way you are, and it might be a help in pointing out the problems or tensions that develop as we go through life. Knowing the characteristics of your particular birth order may help you understand yourself better. Knowing the characteristics of other birth orders may help you understand and get along more easily with others. The result would be a happier life for yourself. It may also help you release into the world some of that life-giving ingredient which you hopefully have received—love not based on or determined by any outer condition or circumstance.

Becky was the first-born in a family of three. Her birth order said she should be a compliant child, highly driven to seek approval, to achieve, and to avoid mistakes. Becky seemed to follow that model. Her parents were members of a church where unconditional love was set forth as an ideal to be realized and practiced. It would be hard to find two more eager parents than Becky's mom and dad when it came to doing all the right things so that Becky would grow up adjusted and whole. From the beginning they consciously expressed their love for Becky in every way they could.

When Becky started school, that love received a new challenge. Becky was now sent daily out of the nest in order to achieve and was brought back home at the end of the day to talk about her achievements. She had all the normal anxieties that any child has in starting school, but she demonstrated that she was an apt and willing pupil in spirit. However, the first graded paper that Becky received on her penmanship did not reflect excellence. Across the top of the paper the teacher had penciled in bold red letters for the parents: *Needs Improvement!* The parents discussed with Becky what that meant and what she needed to do. Becky was quiet and outwardly betrayed no undue concern that her first writings resembled hen scratchings in a barnyard. Inwardly, though, something else was taking place. She sat each evening and laboriously practiced making her letters under the doting eyes of her parents.

Some weeks later Becky brought home another paper. This one had written in red pencil across the top:

Excellent. Shows Much Improvement!! Becky showed the paper to her parents and then queried anxiously, "Now do you love me?"

Her parents were young, but they were wise enough to say, "Becky, we love you no matter what kind of work you do in school. Nothing will ever take away our love for you."

How did this little girl, growing up in a home where love was consciously and generously directed to her every day, have the sense that the love she was receiving was conditional? Could it have had something to do with her birth order, the fact that she was the first-born?

Let's take a glance at the general traits and characteristics of birth order as advanced to us by a number of psychologists and child behavior therapists. This list is not exhaustive nor conclusive, but it does represent what many feel to be the traits that develop in children as a result of where they come in the family line-up.

The Oldest or The First-Born

They are usually achievers, driven toward success in their fields. They tend to be perfectionists and are well organized. They are generally scholarly, serious and critical. They are more often supporters of the law than breakers of it, and they are more inclined to try to please people than to offend them. Since they are believers in authority, they also tend to be legalistic and conservative. While first-borns are good workers and leaders, they have a strong need for approval and therefore organize and perform their work to get praise from parents and later from peers, boss, and spouse.

Why are they this way? Parents are basically responsible. With first-borns, Mom and Dad are just learning what it means to be parents. They tend to operate by the book. They are overprotective and overanxious, while at the same time they can be demanding and pushy. They are always encouraging, whether overtly or covertly, better performance from the child. Because of that, first-borns often become compliant. That does not mean that they are not strong-willed, but they generally learn what pleases Mom and Dad and will do this. First-borns are very much take-charge kinds of persons, because parents have trained them to be little adults. But at the same time they have a compliancy towards spouse or boss, someone who legitimately represents authority. These characteristics go with the first-borns into marriage and influence their behavior. They usually become authoritarian parents.

The big problem of first-borns is pressure. They are often over-disciplined and sometimes over-punished. First-borns will complain that they were more severely restricted than their younger siblings. There is usually truth to this charge.

I am the youngest of three boys. (There is a gap of ten years and fourteen years, respectively, between my younger half brother and half sister and me, which really creates a second family and a whole different set of dynamics, which I will not deal with here.) To this very day, my two older brothers, Dan and Dick (one year apart in age) bring up the fact that they always had to toe the line while Rodney could get away with murder. I don't doubt that this is true, and there is an explanation for it, which we will see when we come to the section on the last-born child.

Another big problem for first-borns is perfectionism. Perfectionists are hard on themselves and everybody else. They are not known for being forgiving. They can nurse grudges for a long time and usually do. Since first-borns grow up with adults as primary role model, they buy strongly into the syndrome of authority figures. Their view of God is often that of a stern judge, a stern lawgiver, or a stern parent. First-borns have a lot of trouble with the concept of unconditional love, for they cannot believe God is big enough to forgive everybody and everything. They are hung up on thinking they have to do something to earn God's forgiveness and love. This is not to say that they cannot grow away from this limiting view, but they do have a special burden inflicted on them by their birth that makes the concept of unconditional love difficult for them to accept and express. Once they see it genuinely demonstrated, however, they, like little Becky, will begin to respond.

The Only Child

Only children are usually lonely children. They tend to be critical of themselves as well as others, and they relate better to adults than to peers. Only children can either be the crown jewel in the family or the scapegoat for parents' frustrations. They usually don't have much of a childhood, because parents tended to treat them like adults from the first. All the labels we apply to first-borns can be applied to only-borns, with one exception: add the word extremely. Only children are extremely perfectionist, extremely reliable, extremely well-organized, extremely cautious, and so forth. The problem is that their standards are so high they often walk close to the precarious edge of discouragement and defeat.

Only-borns can sometimes be a blend of first-borns and last-borns, for that is indeed what they are. So along with other things, they may be pampered and spoiled. Dr. Alfred Adler, who was one of the first to advance birth order as a critical part of psychological development, made a harsh judgment on the only-borns when he said that sooner or later they become useless in life.[12] That's considerably overdrawn. I can think offhand of a number of only children in my own circle of acquaintance who are some of the most useful and loving people I know. Albert Einstein, incidentally, was an only child.

Only children generally need and thrive on time for themselves, because they usually had a lot of it. This makes them excellent candidates for the contemplative modes of life. Though they are often tagged selfish and self-centered, and though they battle with all the pressures of the first-borns, they can still make their birth order work to advantage for them. In their loneliness they achieve something comparable to what one of their pre-cursors of ancient history achieved. Samuel, the only child of Elkanah and Hannah, received a call from God to become a priest. His call came at a dark chapter in Israel's history when religious calls were few and religious devotion was low. Samuel became a significant voice, and sometimes an only voice, reminding the people of their religious heritage and faith. There is still a unique role for only-borns to fulfill in the world today.

The Middle Child

The middle child is the most difficult to describe. Kevin Leman in his book, **The Birth Order,** describes the middle child as born too late and too soon, too late to get the privileges and special treatment of the first-born and too soon to strike the bonanza that many last-borns enjoy.[13] Leman also contends that the middle-born always plays off the first-born. He bounces off the one directly above him and will generally be the opposite.

Many middle-borns don't feel special or particularly wanted. They often feel misunderstood, neglected, and upstaged. They tend to develop their best friends outside the home, and will usually have many friends, in contrast to first-borns, who will have few. They do this to ease the pain of feeling like an interloper in the family and also to ease their own feelings of alienation. The middle-borns are prone to get into gangs that Mom and Dad disapprove of, and they are likely to bring home some of the scruffiest and least desirable kids in town. And watch out for the first one they try to marry; they may deliberately choose someone that is guaranteed to give Mom and Dad coronaries!

Because the world pays less attention to middle children than it does to others, they may be driven to bizarre behavior as a means of getting recognition. Long hair, drugs, alcohol, or other off limits behavior may suddenly make their appearance in the middle-borns of the most circumspect families. It is not uncommon to find many middle-borns alcoholics in their later years.

It sounds as though the middle-borns have three strikes against them before they ever get started, just because of their birth order. But there is another side to it. Middle-borns are often notoriously good mediators and reconcilers. They are generally peacemakers, having learned this skill as a survival technique.

Dick, the middle-born in my family, is our family mediator. He gets along equally well with all members of the family, and it is usually he who mediates any family squabble and calls the family together for reunions and outings. Beverly, my wife and also a middle child, is a born mediator and reconciler. She has the capacity to endure and get along with anyone and always seeks to mediate conflict wherever it arises.

The only problem with mediators is that others sometimes take advantage of them. They can become the victims of manipulative, domineering types, unless they learn how to stand their ground. Middle children can settle for less than perfectionism, because they've learned how to do that from the start. Since their expectations and demands are not as high as first-borns, they are more accepting and more inclined to make do with what they have. However, if the first-born has made an impact as a model, middle-borns may also be afflicted with perfection-ism, at least a degree of it. They can then rise to respon-sible positions of leadership because they understand the principles of compromise and negotiation, as well as the drive to achieve. Being a middle child has helped develop their natural skills to see all sides and to deal com-passionately with everyone.

Middle-borns get my vote for the most natural candidates for both accepting and expressing uncondi-tional love. They have usually learned that comparisons are futile and judgments are pointless. They are willing to listen to others, and they draw few or no barriers in their acceptance and understanding of people. They often emulate the basic principles of unconditional love without even being aware there is such a thing. In many ways, being a middle child, the unheralded, mysterious one that often merits the hand-me-downs and fewer photos in the family album than anyone else, is a position to be envied. It is a birth order that offers the best training for a life of love.

The Youngest, Or The Last-Born

If first-borns are perfectionists, and middle-borns are neglected, what are the last-borns? They are generally spoiled. They are also charmers, manipulators, performers, affectionate, uncomplicated, sometimes theatrical, and often a bit "flaky." Likewise, they can be carefree, vivacious, witty, and adoring. But watch out! The reverse side of that coin occasionally appears, and they can also be rebellious, critical, temperamental, spoiled, and impetuous.

By the time the youngest arrives, parents have usually had it. They used the book for the first one, tried to do the same by the second one, but after that they get "too pooped for any more pedagogy."[14] The youngest is there to be enjoyed rather than disciplined. Naturally, this can occasion some resentment from the older siblings, and the youngest may have to get used to being pampered by his parents and put down by his brothers and sisters. From cuddled and coddled to being curtailed and cut off, they often develop into impetuous and pushy brats. Even after they become adults, they may retain childish behavior, and usually they will feel like the youngest in a group, even when they are not.

Because the youngest-borns like center stage, they often end up in a career that offers them the limelight. (I am the youngest-born of my mother's first family, and I am a minister where center stage is pretty much the order of the day; and that despite the fact I often battle against a crippling sense of shyness and lack of self-confidence). The problem is that youngest-borns often forget that there are others who might like a little of center stage now and then. Youngest-borns also forget to consult with others about their feelings and ideas, and they are slow to give praise, although they depend on it from others. They have a tendency to use people as their audience or as points of reference, rather than as partners in an enterprise of mutual concern. Youngest-borns are generally trained to be self-centered, and many of them expect others to wait on them, having forever been "the baby" of the family.

From my point of view, and maybe because I am one, youngest-borns have the hardest lot. Being last in the line-up creates a lot of problems that nothing but grace and stern self-discipline together can overcome. We last-borns are usually stubborn, determined to lead the way and yet accustomed to somebody being there to pick us up when we fall down. Perhaps that is why I have embraced the concept of unconditional love with such fervor. I know I can never hope to merit it. If I am going to get any, it will have to come free.

Obviously a number of factors have not been considered here, such as the differentials that gender, physical or mental handicaps, age spread, adoption, uneven parental guidance, and other factors can make in the development of children. I have not meant this as anything other than a way of looking at some possibilities that make us the way we are, as well as giving us a depth of understanding about others that will help us love them despite their shortcomings. No birth order fits every mold discussed here, but many do. Moreover, most birth order studies are built on the stereotype of two parents and three children. This is no longer a realistic picture of the American family, where one out of every three households is now headed by a single parent.

Nor have I said much here to relieve the anxiety some parents must feel about raising their children. Being a parent is the most demanding, challenging role we ever take on, and it requires skill, courage, vision, and grace. I think the best thing parents can do for their children is to love each other first and their children second. The most important anchor for any child as he or she is growing up is the love his parents have for each other. Any marriage where the children come ahead of the marriage partners is a deficient marriage. I especially want to stress here in the blended family (where two families come together by the marriage of the parents) that this rule is paramount. If either one of the marriage partners puts his or her kids ahead of the other marriage partner, they are headed for trouble.

Being the product of divorced parents and the participant in a second family, I know something of the pain and trauma a child can feel at that level. But nothing determines our fate unless we allow it. We can break any mold, any pattern, or any restriction that has been placed upon us if we have the will to do so. Children of divorced parents deserve their own study, for their situation is compounded by unusual and traumatic forces. The important thing for them to remember is that forgiveness is the key to their wholeness.

We are told that after age twenty, surface behaviors may change in people but basic level values do not. What early life has taught us to be, we generally are until we die. Only one thing can change the values implanted in us from our early years, and that is what psychologists call a Significant Emotional Event (SEE). A SEE is any experience that has a strong enough influence to shift basic value programming. This can be a severe loss, the entrance of something shattering, revolutionary or traumatic. It can also be the invasion of a great love, which has the capacity to produce total transformation.

A religious conversion is the strongest SEE possible, because it is marked by an onslaught of tremendous love. The call to Christian discipleship is a call to a drastic shift of values and to a universal level of love and concern. It changes us at the deepest level of our being and literally makes us new creatures. A church that teaches and practices unconditional love has the unique potential of reshaping people's basic value systems and altering their responses to live in a dramatic way.

In the final analysis, where we are in our birth family does not matter nearly as much as who we are in terms of the human family. If we know ourselves to be sons and daughters of God, accepted and treasured unconditionally with a universal love, we will be recipients of our true birth inheritance and the bearers of that love to all the members of the human household.

---

[12] Adler, Alfred. **Understanding Human Nature.** New York: Fawcett World Library, 1969, 127.

[13] Leman, Kevin. **The Birth Order.** Old Tappan, New Jersey: Fleming H. Revell, 1984, 72-81.

[14] Leman, *op. cit.,* 85.

Chapter Nine

Stepchildren of God

Approximately 9% of all people in the world are left-handed. There was a time when teachers marched up and down the rows of classrooms in America to spot these oddball aberrations of nature and attempted to train them to be right-handed. Eventually, this method proved futile and was abandoned when it was discovered that it made left-handed people ambidextrous but did not make them right-handed. Left-handed people were then allowed to celebrate their God-given right to be left.

Approximately 9% of all Americans are homosexuals, and that proportion does not differ widely from culture to culture or from one period to another. Since the dawn of religious awareness, we have had guardians of the faith, who, by tactics similar to teachers trying to bend left-handed children into the right-handed mode, have attempted to eradicate homosexuality by branding it an abomination and aberration in the sight of God and nature. All their efforts have failed. Approximately 9% of all people still remain homosexual.

This issue might well be one of the most crucial and divisive faced by the church since the issue of slavery. Today we look back with horror and disbelief that the church ever condoned slavery and branded a people inferior on the basis of their race. Will not some future generation look back at this generation in similar horror and disbelief at our present judgmental and unloving attitudes against homosexuality?

People I care about deeply, including members of my family, will not agree with what I am going to say here. But no discussion of unconditional love can ignore the treatment that society has handed down to this 9% of our population, much of it condoned and led by the Christian church. It is now clear to me that God's unconditional love embraces the whole of humanity, not parts of it. Thus, when God asks us to love all people, God literally meant *ALL* people. I hope I can persuade you to see it that way also. Whether or not you wish to agree with my conclusions about homosexuality, I pray you can agree that they are people who deserve our love and acceptance.

A radical tension exists between common Biblical understanding of homosexuality and the modern consensus of the scientific community. Let's look briefly at what each has to say.

There are comparatively few references to homosexuality in the Bible, and when these do occur, they are usually incidental to other points. The first comes in Genesis 19:1-11, the story of the destruction of the cities of Sodom and Gomorrah. This is a passage often quoted as a divine condemnation of homosexuality.

A careful reading of that passage reveals that the punishment visited upon the cities was not for homosexuality itself but for inhospitality to strangers, lack of concern for the poor, and attempted homosexual gang rape. Some scholars disagree as to whether homosexual activity played any role in the story at all, since the wording is not specific. Certainly, it is not the main theme. We know that a common Middle East practice of this period was to submit captured male foes to anal rape as an expression of domination and scorn. The story, no matter how you look at it, is a poor starting point for a biblical understanding of sexual ethics. The attempted homosexual rape by the men of Sodom (if that is what it was) is explicitly condemned, but Lot's offer to hand over his two virgin daughters to the lusty Sodomites in place of the men is accepted without a word of condemnation.

The next Old Testament passage where homosexuality is mentioned is Leviticus 18:22 and 20:13 in the so-called Holiness Code. These passages give instruction that anyone caught in a homosexual act shall be put to death. By and large, Christians today ignore the Holiness Code with its complex rules for sacrifice and dietary regulations. It takes a highly selective kind of biblical interpretation to choose two verses from the Holiness Code as binding and ignore all the others. Moreover, if the instruction is to be taken literally, we must advocate the death penalty for homosexuality. Can any responsible and caring Christian accept this commandment literally and carry it out?

It is obvious that the early Israelites had an abhorrence of homosexual activity. The Holiness Code was apparently compiled to protect the social and religious fabric of the nation. Certain practices were forbidden because they threatened the network which kept the community together and insured its future. The people of Israel were trying to define themselves against other peoples of Canaan and not be drawn into practices that would ultimately degrade and destroy them as a nation of faith.

When we come to the New Testament, we have to pass over the gospels and go to the Apostle Paul for any word on the subject of homosexuality. Jesus said absolutely nothing on the subject, which is curious. If it was such a big thing, why did he ignore it? The obvious answer is that apparently he did not feel it was important enough to merit comment. Jesus was in the wider business of expanding the concept of neighbor to include everyone, rather than drawing lines of division and hatred. "Love one another" was the thrust of his message, and only where there was blatant disregard for that mandate did he speak to specific issues. His silence on the subject of homosexuality, while not explicit as to approval, can neither be interpreted as condemning. So on to Paul.

The most cited reference in the New Testament letters

of Paul on the subject of homosexuality is in the first chapter of Romans (1:26-27). Here Paul does not simply include homosexual practice as an evil among other evils; he gives a theological rationale for his condemnation as part of a complex argument about salvation. The sin of idolatry, which is giving up the "natural" worship of God for the "unnatural" worship of what is not God, is compared to lust for persons of the same sex. Paul believes this to be unnatural. Although he focuses mainly on the condemnation of idolatry, he views homosexual practices in a negative light and condemns them as a means of strengthening his argument. Paul understands homosexual practices to be God's punishment for the Gentile sin of idolatry. "For this reason God gave them up to dishonorable passions" (Romans 1:26). "And since they did not see fit to acknowledge God, God gave them up to a base mind and to improper conduct" (Romans 1:28). Paul wants to convict the Gentiles of idolatry, not homosexuality. Homosexual activity is a result of idolatry, according to his logic. Such practices are not the cause of God's wrath, but the outcome of it. Moreover, it is clear that he understands homosexual activity as that indulged in by heterosexuals, and it is this factor that makes the practice unnatural in his eyes.

Paul's other references to this subject are 1 Corinthians 6:9-10 and 1 Timothy 1:8-11. Here he simply includes homosexual acts in lists of practices that dishonor God and harm one's neighbor.

There is no question that Paul plainly condemns homosexual acts. Indeed, all the biblical passages on the subject deal with it on pretty much the same level. But note carefully that nowhere does the Bible say anything about homosexuality as a sexual orientation. It is always an activity indulged in by those who are supposedly heterosexual.

Paul's argument that homosexual practices are the punishment one receives for idolatry is not particularly compelling to us today. It is true that idolatry, the dishonoring of God, inevitably results in the dishonoring of persons, but this is as much a heterosexual concern as a homosexual one. We must not forget that Paul, for all his brilliance and peerless commitment, was a human person, subject to error and conditioned by his culture. Surely if we dare question his opinions about the social status of women and the institution of slavery, we might also dare question his perceptions of homosexuality.

If one insists on a literal obedience to the Bible, then we would all need to change our diets, get behind capital punishment, support the reinstitution of slavery, and stone homosexuals to death. Paul himself does not follow such a narrow line of reasoning. He vigorously argues that the Christian is justified not by law but by faith. He insists that God's favor is not something we earn by what we do; rather, it is a free gift. He suggests that we guard against using our new freedom as an opportunity for the flesh, and "through love be servants of one another" (Galatians 5:13). The test of whether a Christian is faithful is not by obedience to the law, but by the ability to turn to one another in love. If we are then in a right relationship to God solely because of God's grace, we need to let go of our efforts to castigate homosexuals and instead serve them in love. The biblical message may be muddled on the matter of homosexuality, but the gospel's mandate to love is crystal clear.

Those today who condemn homosexuality as a sin do so on the basis that the Bible teaches it is unnatural and a violation of God's command. The Bible, however, condemns certain types of homosexual behavior; it does not explicitly condemn homosexuality. Is not the central theme of the gospel God's overwhelming love in Jesus Christ and God's willingness to forgive anything we offer to him in faith and repentance? The uncertain area of this discussion is whether or not homosexuality is a sin (something knowingly selected) or a condition of life (something not chosen which must therefore be accepted). If it is a sin, it needs forgiveness. If it is a biological fact, it needs acceptance.

The great majority of homosexuals say they did not indeed have a choice concerning their sexual orientation, any more than do heterosexuals. Although we have been inclined to dismiss this statement with a what-do-they-know attitude, we have had to agree there is no certain conclusion about the causes of homosexuality. In 1973 the trustees of the American Psychiatric Association did delete homosexuality from their list of mental disorders saying, "Homosexuality *per se* implies no impairment in judgment, stability, reliability, or general social or vocational capabilities." Prior to that, homosexuality had officially been looked upon as a mental illness.

In 1984 researchers on the subject came forth with the statement that they now have the first clear evidence of a biological difference between homosexual and heterosexual men, a dissimilar response to hormones that may have developed before birth. In measuring rising and falling levels of hormones due to stimulation by other hormones, scientists found that the responses of homosexual men fell between those of heterosexual men and women.

This new research, done at the State University of New York at Stony Brook by Dr. Brian Gladue, chief researcher, and Drs. Richard Green and Ronald Hellman, and reported in the prestigious journal **Science,** is landmark evidence pointing to the possibility of biological markers for homosexual orientation. This difference to the responses of hormone levels to certain stimulation is consistent with previous research showing that prenatal hormonal influences in mammals affect lifelong sexual orientation. If it is really a question of biology, a matter over which people have no real choice, what does this do to our judgments? Is there some rent in our genetic fabric that is creating this aberration, or is it just a part of God's intention and an additional challenge to our ability to love as God does?

Who knows? Certainly I do not. But it is my own deep

belief in the fundamental value of all persons that leads me to favor the full acceptance of homosexuals. Nor would I deny them the right to express affection in the same self-less manner I would hope heterosexuals would express it. Homosexuals desire deep and lasting relationships just as much as heterosexuals, and appropriate sexual expression should be allowed for both. We do not have full truth, and we must live with that tension. We can continue to share our wonderings, but we cannot continue to deny each other love and still be participants in the life of unconditional love into which God invites all of us. Nor can we mouth the platitude, "God loves the homosexual but hates homosexuality.:" The missing logic in such a statement is self-evident and hardly perorative.

What about accepting homosexual Christians into our churches? Some of my colleagues in the ministry, whom I respect, have told me that they will not allow avowed homosexuals to be members of their churches. The underlying assumption seems to be that as long as they don't know about it, it doesn't matter, but once it's out in the open, they have to say "no."

It grieves me that such attitudes are still strong among professional church leaders. It not only reflects a bias that is nearly as outdated as believing that whites are superior to blacks, it also encourages deception and dishonesty.

I favor the full acceptance of homosexual Christians into the ongoing life of a congregation, and many, many clergy in this country feel likewise. Jesus turned away no one who came to him in faith. Why should we? Nor do we have a right to place any demands upon their sexuality that we would not place on ourselves. Homosexual people have suffered and hurt and waited long enough. They have borne great pain all of their lives. We have no right to add to that pain. We have only the right to love and bless them and to help them live out their own humanity in the way they feel God is calling them.

Prejudice in all its forms is abhorrent and falls short

of the norm of Christian morality. Prejudice against homosexuals is a greater violation of the gospel and the norm of Christian morality than is any homosexual orientation or activity. All forms of prejudice are an affront to the dignity of persons, and yet churches across this country have contributed to the maintenance of an environment that is prejudicial to homosexuals. The church is seriously obliged to work toward the eradication of these and all prejudices.

Dr. Charles Z. Smith, past President of the American Baptist Churches, an esteemed judge and lawyer in the city of Seattle and a valued member of my present church, said to the General Board of the American Baptist Churches in 1977: "We must intelligently and thoughtfully explore in open discussion and debate the subject of human sexuality and its component, homosexuality, in the context of the Christian life. . . . We cannot continue to sweep the issue of homosexuality under the rug. I do not believe there are stepchildren in the Family of God."

A once faceless minority called homosexuals is now emerging into men and women we see every day. They are precious human beings, members of the family of humankind, part of the world God created and sustains and deeply loves. They are fully loved by God, they wait to be loved by us and to give their love in return. They are our brothers and sisters. The task of loving them, even though we may not fully understand them, is now before us. The task may confuse us and call for a compromise on our old convictions. We shall certainly cry out to God for wisdom and courage, but we cannot turn back. We have come too far on the path of unconditional love to turn back now. To be thrust into the stream where we are asked to declare every man a brother and every woman a sister may be intimidating, but such broad concerns are part of the higher way of love.

Chapter 10

Unconditional Love In Nature

One warm summer afternoon Beverly and I were walking through a mountain meadow. There was a rustle in a grove of willows as we passed by, and suddenly from that copse dashed a deer in full flight, directly across our paths. No sooner was the deer out of sight than another creature ran out from the grove. It was a fawn, a little baby whose legs still wobbled unsteadily. Without a moment's hesitation, it lurched in our direction and stopped before us, nose quivering and ears twitching. He waited beside us trustingly, too young to recognize possible danger.

My first impulse was to reach down and caress the fawn. Then, remembering the frantic dash of that mother across our trail and realizing that she had deliberately been trying to draw us away from her little one, even to the point of offering her own life if necessary, I refrained. Quietly we withdrew from the meadow, knowing the doe would quickly come back and claim her little one. There was no need, it seemed to me, to leave my scent on the creature which she prized more highly than herself.

I felt in that brief, shining moment not unlike Loren Eiseley, who described tusseling with a baby fox over a bone on a sand dune as an opportunity to view the universe from its front side. He said the universe presented its face to him in the friendly innocence of a baby fox, and it was such a glorious revelation that it seemed to him the universe itself was laughing.

We humans often find our most treasured and meaningful moments in nature. Is it not because nature is our teacher, offering us the handbook that will guide us to the truth of our own being, if we only have the sensitivity and wisdom to read it correctly? Oh, I know that nature has its violent and cruel side, that it can become the tyrant and the destroyer in an instant. But then, so can we humans when our true instincts are perverted.

It is said that at the beginning of the twentieth century, after the buffalo had practically been exterminated by the slaughter of the whites, one buffalo wandered across the prairie not far from a small town in Wyoming. The townspeople hitched up their wagons and rode out to see what the creature looked like. They drove around the animal with their wagons, forming a circle with the buffalo inside. For a long time they stared at this legendary animal whose precursors had once dotted the plains of this continent but which was now nearly extinct. Then, because they could not imagine what else to do, somebody shot it.

Paul writes in the eighth chapter of Romans that creation groans in travail, waiting in eager longing for the revealing of the sons (and daughters) of God. He sees this travail as something subjected upon creation by the Creator in hope, the hope that as we humans achieve maturity as the children of God, creation will be set free. This is not unlike the vision of the prophet Isaiah who saw into the future to the establishment of a peaceful kingdom to be marked by the wolf dwelling with the lamb, the leopard lying down with the goat, the calf with the lion, while the cow and the bear grazed together. "And the suckling child shall play over the hole of the asp, and the weaned child shall put his hand on the adder's den. They shall not hurt or destroy in all my holy mountain." (Isaiah 11:6-9) Isaiah further described the vision with mountains and hills breaking forth into singing, and all the trees of the field clapping their hands (Isaiah 55:12-13).

The writers of the Bible knew there was a correlation

between human destiny and fate of all creation. Not only does nature portray the laws of God clearly, it is linked to us in such a way that what we do to it, we do to ourselves.

Ernesto Cardenal says that "all nature is oriented toward a 'thou' and that all things that are alive are in communion with each other."[16] He points to the phenomenon of mimesis, whereby all plants, animals and all beings are fraternally united in mimicry. "There are insects which mimic flowers and flowers which act like insects, animals which resemble water or rocks or desert sand or snow or woodland or certain other animals. And thus all beings love each other or feed each other, and all are united in a gigantic process of birth and growth and reproduction and death."[17]

Nature always seeks to replace desolation with renewal, to transcend its own limitations and go beyond the limits of its own individuality. It is always trying to meet its own "I" with a "thou," to which it can give itself and by which it can be transformed. All the laws of nature are essentially manifestations of the Supreme Law of Love. The poets have instinctively grasped at the love manifest in nature by speaking of being caressed by the wind, kissed by the sun, guided by the stars, etc. Our language instinctively proclaims that we are part of nature and that nature is part of us, and that we are all uniting and separating and then uniting again under a force and rhythm called love.

Who can doubt the presence of unconditional love in nature who has ever owned a dog, a cat or any other pet? Perhaps the dog demonstrates it best of all. A dog is absolutely willing to be whatever its owner decrees it shall be, and it will respond in loyal devotion to even the most hideous and horrible human, if affection and devotion have been bestowed on it. I have never owned goldfish or turtles, and I have absolutely no interest in ever trying to make a pet of a snake or a spider of any kind or description. Yet I am told by those who have an affinity for those creatures and who have worked with them, that they will show signs of affection for their owner if the owner is consistent in giving the same. Nor is it an affection conditioned solely on the basis that the owner is the provider of food; rather it is an affection for affection's sake.

I have occasionally amused my congregation by telling stories of the crow who calls my name when I go out in my yard, or the snake who lived in my garden for several years and crawled to my door to die. Yet I know there is virtually no one who does not instinctively yearn for connectedness and unification with all life. I believe that unification can come if it is a sincere longing and if we work at it earnestly.

My wife likes spiders. When she finds them in the house, she picks them up and carries them outside, and they never appear to be frightened or concerned. Try though I might, I am not as fond of spiders as I ought to be. In fact, big spiders scare me purple. Whenever I try to help one outside, usually armed with gloves, handkerchief, glass jar, etc., I end up frightening the creature so badly it does its best to get away from me and often gets injured in the process. It is the difference of what is inside, and I cannot hide it. Fear is communicated just as clearly as love to all forms of life.

Hannah Hurnard, the English mystic who believes that if we harm nothing we shall be harmed by nothing, once told of stopping beneath a giant tree, looking upward at its spreading branches, and asking, "What is your secret, O tree? How can I grow old as gracefully and as beautifully as you have done?" To which she purports the tree gave her instruction to do three things: (1) look up to the light; (2) welcome all who come to you for refuge and care; (3) be willing to let go of things at the right time. "If you do this, as I have done," said the tree, "you shall grow old beautifully and gracefully and will always be a blessing to the world."

Whether Hannah Hurnard's tree talked to her, or whether it was the unfolding of a spiritual truth within her own consciousness, the instructions are peerless in their wisdom. Here is the path towards unconditional love: keep your face lifted up to God each day; receive with warmth and love all those who come to you; at the right time relinquish the old to make way for the new. How gloriously that lesson is portrayed by the tree who lifts its branches each day to the light of God, who receives any who pause beneath it or on its branches, and who, at the right season in the predestined cycle of things, lets go of the old leaves in order to prepare the way for the new.

Thomas Merton, a Trappist monk, said, "A tree gives glory to God by being a tree. For in being what God means it to be, it is obeying him. It 'consents,' so to speak, to his creative love. It is expressing an idea which is in God and which is not distinct from the essence of God, and therefore, a tree imitates God by being a tree."

All things give glory to God by being what they have been created to be. All things speak to us of God. The entire creation proclaims eloquently the existence, the majesty, the beauty and the love of God. God's name is the signature placed on all things, and all creatures, animate or inanimate, are messages to us of God's love. If some choose to label this notion as sentimental drivel, so be it. The world has little enough sentiment in these mad, risky, speeded-up times in which we live. When we contemplate the brute truth that the rope of the final curtain of history is in the hands of short-sighted men who might choose to ring down the end of the planetary drama at any moment, it's enough to scare us to death, or else to scare us to love.

There is little to be gained by dwelling on the rueful and bloody pages of past history, except as a means to learn where we went wrong and to avoid repeating our mistakes. Much can be learned, though, by studying the patterns of life and religious thought of the Native Americans of this continent, whom we betrayed with treaties, forced onto reservations, and nearly eradicated no less cruelly than we did the buffalo. The Indians felt that the supreme diety had a plan for the earth, and that we belonged to the earth rather than the earth belonging to us. They thought nature was created for everybody and failed to understand why individuals or groups should appropriate it for themselves and deplete its resources through wanton slaughter and careless usage. There are far too many chapters in the past when we humans, destined to express the essence of God, failed to do so. We have much yet to learn, and nature is patiently waiting to teach us, if we do not succeed in destroying it first.

I have an eighty-year-old friend in Scotland named Margaret who has a rare sensitivity to the animal world. She has shared with me some real-life parables, one of which I choose to share with you now.

In the fall, Scottish farmers would gather to help one another move the small stacks of hay from the fields into barns. Because rats made their homes in these stacks, and because rats were destroyers of the crops, the farmers and older children carried poles and boards with which they clubbed the rats to death as they ran from under the stacks. It was a brutal, gruesome ritual, but little Margaret, only eight years old at the time, had been taught to accept it, even though she did not wish to participate in it.

One day, midway through this sorry but necessary carnage, came a strange event. As a small stack was lifted to be placed on the wagon, three rats were discovered crouched together. They did not run as the others had. Instead, they began to walk slowly as a trio, sides touching sides, moving with a kind of painful dignity across the stubbled fields. As the men watched, clubs upraised, they noted that the middle rat was sightless. Its eyes were sealed over by a membrane. The blind rat was being led away by the other two.

Little Margaret, watching nearby, felt her eyes fill with tears over the loving sacrifice of the rats for each other and began to pray, "O God, let them go." The men and children observing that humble and lowly processional of three rats spoke not a word. And not a club was lowered against them. The rats were allowed to move out into the open fields in search of a new place of refuge and safety.

We always have a choice about whether to be compassionate or not. There is an essential goodness in people which usually helps them make the choice in favor of love, if that goodness can be touched and uncovered. That is what nature is trying to do for us. That is what we are meant to do for each other.

---

[15] Eiseley, Loren. **The Unexpected Universe.** New York: Harcourt Brace Jovanovich, Inc., 1964, 204-212.

[16] Cardenal, Ernesto. **To Live Is To Love.** New York: Doubleday, 1971, 23.

[17] *Ibid.*

Chapter Eleven

A Theology Of Blessing

There has been a tendency down through the years to depict a great gulf between God and the world. Traditionally the world has been viewed as depraved and at war with God. It is interesting that while this belief has sprung full-blown from Christianity, the creation narratives that fill the first chapters of the Bible deny that gulf. In the first two chapters of Genesis, God stands not over against the world but alongside and in friendly continuity with it. The world itself is seen as a vehicle for the blessings God has ordained in it as a continuing and abiding characteristic.

Three times in the first two chapters of Genesis the term "blessing" is used: of living creatures (1:22), of human creatures (1:28), and of the sabbath as a day of rest (2:3). The attitude of God towards creation is summed up in the final verse of the first chapter: "And God saw everything that he had made, and behold, it was very good."

Blessing theology affirms that the world was blessed at the first moment of its creation, and that God is continuing to bless it. Despite all our wrongdoings and unfaithfulness to our Creator God, the Creator continues to delight in creation as it was created. God will neither abandon nor withdraw its original permit of freedom. This is a revolutionary thought. To affirm a theology of blessing voices a protest against many of the alternative ideologies of our time. That protest might best be depicted by a chart showing the major distinctions between the doctrine of original sin and the doctrine of original blessing. Here I am indebted to Matthew Fox and his landmark book, **Original Blessing,** for bringing these distinctions into focus.

Original Sin	Original Blessing
The world is essentially evil and hostile to God.	The world is essentially good, deriving its goodness from its Creator.
God is an outsider to the world.	God is at work in the world to bring about its divine purpose.
All humans are sinners and only a faithful few will be saved.	All humans are holy sons and daughters of God, whose major sin is forgetting who they are.
Faith is assenting to God's inscrutable demands.	Faith is trusting God with one's full being.
Salvation is personal only.	Salvation is both personal and corporate; the healing of the soul is part of the greater work of healing the cosmos.
The world will be destroyed because it is evil.	The world is destined for consummation and fulfillment.
Death is the wages of sin, an enemy to be feared.	Death is the normal outcome to life, a door to rebirth.

The list could go on, but you can begin to see the difference. A theology of blessing stresses a growing process towards fulfillment rather than a closed system. The Genesis account encourages human creatures "to be fruitful" and "to have dominion" over all the world. We are given dominion over unrealized potentials, which we are responsible for bringing forth. When we do this, we bless the world. This speaks of the most important concepts of our being: we are blessed, and we are destined in love to be a blessing to everything.

What does blessing mean? Matthew Fox says that God loves creation, like any parent loves its children, and that love, which is an unconditional sending forth into existence, is blessing. Blessing is synonymous with unconditional love. God's blessing is a gift of God's divine favor and unmerited grace, a love without conditions. Our blessing of God takes many forms of grateful adoration, one of the most important being worship. When we come to church, it should be to bless God with our gifts and our gratitude, principally because God has blessed us in a similar way. Then we are sent forth into the world to bless it with the joy and the healing that God has given us.

I don't mean to sound like ours is a perfect world, free of sin, and that love is all around us, like a pea soup fog, making everything warm and shivery at the same time. Our world is a broken, torn and sinful place, and love is in high demand, mainly because love, in its unconditioned form, is in short supply. The reasons for that are clear. We have lived separated from God. We have forgotten who we are. When we remember that we are holy sons and daughters of a living, loving God, we can begin the work of healing our separation and simultaneously begin the work of healing our world. Prayer, as I have indicated earlier, is a place where we begin that work of remembering and healing.

We all wonder at one time or another why God didn't create a perfect world in the first place. Well, God did create a perfect world, but its perfection is not yet fully realized or expressed. God left the world incomplete that we, God's immortal children, might feel the challenge and work cooperatively in putting the pieces of the puzzle together. God left the music unsung, the poetry unwritten, and the drama unacted, that there might be a challenge to the mystic human soul to create and bring forth. God also left the ore in the mines, the electricity in the clouds, and the atom in the earth, that we might discover these and learn to use them for our highest good.

Yes, even the atom, locked in the earth since the dawn of its creation, has been placed there for our good. Since 1939 scientists and physicists had believed that a nuclear chain reaction, liberating enormous amounts of energy, could be produced. They did not know whether it could be controlled, or whether those who tried it would be blasted to bits. The project was carried on in Chicago by a brilliant array of scientists who had built a nuclear reactor in a squash court beyond a football stadium. On December 2, 1942, atomic energy was produced, kept under control, and stopped. On that day the world changed. We entered into the age of the greatest physical power the world had ever known.

Three years later, in 1945, several things happened that should never be forgotten. The United States dropped atomic bombs on two Japanese cities, ostensibly to end World War II; and my little hometown of Arco in the desert of southeastern Idaho became the first town in the world to be lighted by atomic energy. It is a long journey from Hiroshima and Nagasaki, Japan to tiny Arco, Idaho, USA, not only in miles and size, but in ideology. The stab of brilliant light that blazed across those cities introduced a new age for humanity, an age of unparalleled anxiety and an age of unprecedented anticipation. We suddenly had on our hands both a devastating weapon of destruction and an instrument of amazing hope.

It has been more than forty years since those events. Both the United States and the Soviet Union now have massive arsenals of nuclear weapons, and our international environment seems to grow more threatening each day. Is there a way into the future that will restrain any more Hiroshimas and Nagasakis and promote more Arcos?

The atomic age has stirred the scientific world to a new sense of moral values and social responsibility, just as it has stirred the religious world to an awareness and appreciation for science. More than any other force, nuclear energy has brought scientists and religious thinkers together in a shared sense of oneness and reverence for the universe. It is true that the arms race is a destructive use of science, just as the doctrine of original sin is a destructive use of religion. But many good effects have resulted from the development of nuclear energy. If we can express our gratitude to God for another great gift and search for the love and wisdom to use this gift carefully and creatively, we can turn the nuclear age into the numenous age.

The atom has stirred people to the need of living together or not living at all. Love is no longer a luxury, it is a necessity, for it is only as we grow into greater consideration of each other that we will be able to achieve the full reward of this age, an age that is paradoxically filled with unlimited peril as well as unlimited promise.

A theology of blessing can rescue us at this point, for it says that God blesses creation rather than condemns it and that everything that is here is here for our good, if we can learn to make wise and loving choices. A theology of blessing means that love, not will power or coercion, is how people and society are most deeply transformed. This makes war a violation of the deepest fabric of creation, as well as a violation of our own essential being.

As one pushes on through the book of Genesis, there is met an account in the narrative that is commonly known as "the fall." But the Genesis account is not primarily concerned with the power of sin or the fall of Adam and Eve. It is primarily concerned with the God of blessing who calls all creatures to live in this world on divine terms. The Bible does not assume that the fall is inevitable or permanently binding; it rather assumes that humankind can indeed obey the purposes of God and that sin is not inevitable. The theme of the Bible is "a God of blessing" and not "the hopeless human predicament." The entire Bible is unitive in this theme, affirming that God is powerful enough to resolve any kind of alienation. This leaves us with the faith that God is at work every day, renewing creation and blessing it.

The life of Jesus Christ epitomizes a theology of blessing at its highest and its deepest. His life represents the greatest spiritual journey ever undertaken. Jesus was willing to let go of life, to confront the fear of death head on, that he might be liberated from everything except unconditional love. The life of Jesus was a dramatic portrayal of one who was willing to let go and let God be God, and it is a radical instruction for us to do the same.

This letting go is a necessary discipline, if we are to experience the full blessing of God. We must let go of our anxieties, our concerns over trivial matters, our fears and our projections, our desires for attention, and most of all, our censorious judgments. We must, in short, let go of our human wills and seek God's will. The powerful image of Jesus praying earnestly in the Garden of Gethsemane for the cup to pass from him, but then ending with the resolve, "Nevertheless, not my will but thine be done," is a summons to let our wills be so emptied that they become the divine will, the divine blessing.

Thomas Merton said, "I must learn to let go of the familiar and the usual and consent to what is new and unknown to me. I must learn to 'leave myself' in order to find myself by yielding to the love of God."

Paul Tournier, the well-known psychologist, once told a patient to let go of his life by giving up directing it. "Stop trying to push it along yourself," said Tournier. When the patient protested that it sounded like renunciation, Tournier replied, "It is renunciation. It is a renunciation for love and not for fear. It is not denying yourself fulfillment, but giving up depending on yourself to attain it."

Life is essentially an obligation, not a privilege. It is a task, not a game. It is a duty, not a favor. Most of all, life is a blessing, not a burden. When life is received as a blessing, the obligation becomes a privilege, the task turns into a pleasure, and the duty is translated into joy.

Our highest destiny is to let God find us and shape us into what we are meant to be. Our highest work is to bless creation in the same manner God blesses it. Thus, the glory of our devotion to God becomes a treasure on earth, and through us, the disciples of unconditional love, God is able to love the world back to its divine image, its original good.

Chapter Twelve

Cosmogenesis

The aim of unconditional love is the conquest of all creation. Life is not simply a matter of organizing the earth to serve human needs and increase our sense of well-being. Rather, it is a bringing about a complete refashioning of nature, a transformation of the world that will extract from it all the truth, energy and love that the world potentially holds.

The idea of transformation (a turning about, metamorphosis, transfiguration) is at the heart of both Old and New Testament teachings. Jesus said he had not come to abolish the law and the prophets but to fulfill them. He was primarily concerned with the destiny of the entire universe and not merely the salvation of the individual. His being, expressed through his thoughts and teachings, reached out towards the consummation of the mystical body of creation with a destiny by which it might rise to newness of life. Thus, in Christ we proceed "towards a new heaven and a new earth" through a transforming process, a re-casting effort that moves towards convergence and the unification of all things.

In the New Testament the ultimate aim of Christ's redeeming work is represented as nothing less than cosmic renewal—the transformation of the world in all its communal or social groupings and relationships. This consummation was variously represented as "the coming Day of the Lord," "the Coming of the Son of Man," "the

Second Coming," or "the return of Christ in glory." It was also represented as "the uniting of all things in heaven and on earth," although traditionally this line of thought has not been as popular as the others mentioned. Let us briefly consider this long expected consummation in light of the various guises under which it has evolved.

It is true that the conviction that Christ's return was imminent colored many of the early New Testament writings. The first three gospels, especially Mark, refer to a complex of events in the future, a coming of Christ "with power" and a sweeping away of all barriers to the advancement of a heavenly kingdom. This event would herald the end of an old age and the coming of a new one.

In the Fourth Gospel, however, Jesus's prediction of a return is represented as an abiding spiritual presence rather than a spectacular visible return. This presence came to be recognized by the apostles and early church as the secret and power of the Christian life. This sent them out to conquer the Graeco-Roman world with the revolutionary message of love and to advance the kingdom of Christ in all the relationships of life. It was clear to the later thinkers of the faith that this kingdom was a spiritual one and that its coming was a spiritual process whereby Christ would come more fully into the world as he entered more totally into the hearts of humankind.

When we move to Paul's writings, the description of the event becomes more graphic. Paul foresaw trumpets blowing, graves giving up their dead, and the Son of Man coming on clouds of glory. But Paul's initial expectations were doomed to disappointment, for he believed this would all take place very soon and in his own lifetime. When it did not, he seemingly abandoned the view of a cataclysmic, immediate return and began to see it in terms of a future cosmic event. A spirit of optimism begins to pervade Paul's writings at this point with strong strains of universalism. He moves away from the pessimistic Graeco-Roman view which had first been dominant to the wider idea of a spiritual consummation of history.

But early in church history, when Augustine introduced the doctrine of original sin, the view developed that the Christ event—the life, death and resurrection of Jesus Christ—was the great watershed event to which other previous events led and from which subsequent events followed. The Jew continued to retain the belief that the turning point of history was in the future, but for the Christian it was predominantly in the past. Still the view of a Victory Day in the future could not be fully excised. History was moving somewhere to some culmination point. The scriptures said so. But where? What?

We are left today with a mish-mash of views on eschatology, or the doctrine of future things. The one thing Christians have agreed on is that ultimately this consummation is not dependent on human effort but on God. The general conclusion is that when we talk about the Second Coming or a consummation of history, we are face to face with boundless possibilities but we do not know exactly what these are. It would be contrary to Christian humility and love to set a limit to the wonders of God's guidance of world history, so although the belief has persisted, the details remain unclear. Nevertheless, faith in some kind of eternal consummation at a future point in history has never really deserted Christian or Jewish thought.

We have now reached a point in human development where it is time to lay aside the old fall/redemption tradition, which is not basically scriptural and which considers all nature as fallen and basically evil. We have been following that path for centuries, and it has gotten us nowhere but into confusion. It is time now to come back to the truth of the Bible, that all creation flows from a single, loving source, God, and that all creation is both blessed and a blessing. On its natal day, God bestowed upon creation the original inheritance of love, not sin.

A number of contemporary thinkers and writers, including Walter Brueggemann and Matthew Fox, to mention only two, have set the stage for our starting point to a more liberating view of the future. Neither deny that ours is a sinful world in need of redemption, for that is indeed the biblical thrust, but they insist that we do not enter the world as blotches on existence, as sinful creatures. We burst into the world as blessings of love. So the point from which we must begin our consideration of the goal of creation must be from the point of original blessing and not original sin.

It was Augustine who gave us the doctrine of original sin, a doctrine that has contributed considerably more to sin than it ever took away. In Augustinian thinking the cosmos is evil and not to be trusted. His preoccupation with law, sin and personal salvation all but destroyed any sense of social justice and world responsibilities for centuries.

The doctrine of original sin gave support to the formation of an ecclesiastical hierarchy in the church, because it fostered the notion of the church as an empire, aligned with the state and holding power over the people. The doctrine of original sin played into the hands of slave traders, white supremacists, and male demigods, perpetuating racial oppression and subjugation of women. The doctrine of original sin built a religion almost exclusively around sin and redemption and omitted the supreme values of love and trust. It reawakened the heresy of Docetism, the second century movement led by Marcion and followed by the Gnostics, which said Jesus was entirely God, a phantom who only seemed to be human. In subtle ways, the original sin idea has kept Docetism alive by denying Jesus his humanity, his humanness, that necessary aspect of his being through which his divinity was realized. This can be measured today in the preaching of fundamentalists who speak of Jesus as though he were indeed God and who talk about God as an avenging deity rather than a loving Parent.

The guilt, self-doubt and distrust that have been kept going by the preachment of original sin have left no room for any consideration of a cosmic spirituality or a cosmic blessing. The sense of a cosmic Christ has been almost lost in the West, and the result has been crippling to all of us. Otto Rank, the famed psychoanalyst and contemporary of Sigmund Freud, observed that "when religion lost the cosmos, society became neurotic and had to invent psychology to deal with the neurosis."

A group called Fundamentalist Anonymous (FA) has recently appeared on the American scene. It is a nationwide network of support groups for disillusioned and former fundamentalist Christians. FA asserts that the cultlike aspects of fundamentalism and its preoccupation with sin emotionally scar believers and have proved to be hazardous to the psychological well-being of millions. The group tries to help people work free from the guilt and fear inherent in the fundamentalist experience and to achieve confidence, independence, open-mindedness and an ability to think critically. FA maintains respect for the right of people to their various religious beliefs and does not even claim to be anti-fundamentalist. It is just saying it hasn't worked in their lives, and it hasn't worked for a lot of people. FA hopes to provide an alternative to those who can no longer deal with the intolerance and coercion of fundamentalism but who don't want to give up on the spiritual quest.

Original sin, as expressed in our generation by the fundamentalist movement, has overlooked the fact that people in the deepest sense are social beings. It is our relationships that demand healing, not just our souls. The Kingdom of God is the kingdom of right relationships, and this includes our relationship to the world and our universe. By making the full connections in our lives with all creation, we are ready to move to cosmic spirituality.

A cosmic spirituality is a justice spirituality, for it cares when things are not in harmony and balance, and it works to get the universe straightened out. A cosmic spirituality is also an ecumenical spirituality, in the truest sense of that word, for it sees the essential oneness in every religious path. It recognizes that whether we are a Christian or a Buddhist or a Jew or a Hindu simply depends on when and where we were born, not on the intrinsic content of this or that faith. A cosmic spirituality is a doctrine of unconditional love, for it is a system built on saving the future rather than on some mythical past state of moral perfection.

The key thinker in cosmic spirituality is undoubtedly Pierre Teilhard de Chardin. He developed a series of axioms that appealed to him and which helped him build his dream of the consummation of the universe: *God creates by uniting—to be created is to be united—to be more is for more to be united by more.* He struggled to define a spiritual attitude towards the future for which there was no adequate model from the past, and he came up with the term "cosmogenesis."

Cosmogenesis means the universe is continually growing, a new world is developing. Cosmogenesis is essentially the unification of all things in the universe.

Teilhard's faith in Jesus Christ was as complete as it was ardent and firm, yet he seemed called to go beyond positions generally accepted by the church. He explored spiritual truths which stretched like continents untrodden by human minds, and he gave birth to an authentic witness to Jesus Christ which our world sorely needs. He saw the evolutionary process of creation in Christ as progressing towards greater consciousness, freedom and purpose, and he knew it was our destiny to share in that process. Our assignment was to be co-creators with God for the future of the whole, for cosmogenesis.

Unconditional love leads us to the ultimate realization that we are cosmic creatures with a cosmic responsibility. We are part of the universe that rejects the dualism of heaven and earth and who believes that the Kingdom of God is destined to come on earth, as it is in heaven. A cosmic spirituality is not hung up on a second coming of Jesus, when his first coming has yet to be fully appropriated. But it is aware of a consummation point in history when the universe itself shall be healed and transformed. This great and final mystery, which will be brought about by Jesus Christ, will amount to the creation of a new world, but it will be so radical that it will defy all our methods of investigation or analysis. All we can do is wait for it in hope and confidence.

A doctrine of unconditional love, which claims that love will have final victory over all that love has created, is totally compatible with the idea of cosmogenesis, a universe expanding in love. If creation was blessed by God and given as a blessing, it stands to reason that this blessing will be fulfilled. God will ultimately complete that which God has begun. In Jesus Christ we see the synthesis of the created order with its Creator. When this synthesis or union is expressed, the result is transformation. The more profound the synthesis, the higher the transformation. The result is cosmogenesis, the growth of the universe.

Creation is ever evolving towards greater consciousness, freedom and order. The negative images of the future (Armageddon, nuclear holocaust, social anarchy, communist takeover, etc.) all speak of social breakdown. These are in conflict with the highest biblical picture and at odds with what we humans need in order to grow to our highest potential. We need a new set of positive values and beliefs that will nurture our transformation rather than destroying it. Each of us is a microcosm of the whole, and each of us is needed for spiritual evolution to take place on all levels.

We are affecting the future at this very moment by the way we love or do not love. If we can take on a love for the world and help free people from want of any kind, we will help solve the gigantic social problems that face us. If we can take on a love for nature and help free creation from its bondage of travail, we will help solve the threatening breakdown of our ecological system. If we can take on a love for the universe and begin exploration of the unlimited frontiers of space in cooperation with other nations, rather than setting up defense systems against them, we will unleash a new era of peace on a cosmic scale. Our problems are deep and disturbing, but they all have their solution in love, a love without conditions.

As Barbara Marx Hubbard, futurist and writer, has said, earth bound history is over; the final chapter has been written and the first chapter of cosmic history is already underway. We have been born into the most marvelous and tremendous moment in human history. We can make it, and we will, if we can simply remember that we are one, we are whole, we are love.

The future belongs to those who can give to the next generation the will to love.

Chapter Thirteen

Meditations on Love and Spirituality

I sat one late afternoon in front of my house and watched a brilliant westering sun play with the waters of the Puget Sound until it made the waves translucent, roiling with beauty like a thousand silver salmon swimming beneath their surface. Those waves, careening towards me across a watery meadow with all its shapes and growings, seemed to take on the quality of an infinite font of flickering, broken wings. Alone, upon my sun-drenched promontory, my heart welled up in giddy praise at that moment of grace. I never merited it, could not begin to, yet it pressed its particles of silver and gold at my feet in a steady refrain of remorseless buoyancy. Then the water moved from my feet and began to explode over my head, flinging the air with a perfume, sweeter still than daphne, capturing all my senses and dissolving heaven into that sunspot radiance of water and light. It was a message as threadbare as a lacy curtain in an Andrew Wyeth painting, yet the freshest news I had heard all day. *Here is Love!* What a delightful discovery to become aware once again of the gifts of grace that come from beyond our knowing or control and that shout to us in such eager, waking tones, urging us on towards incarnation with the great creative urge.

●　●　●

There is no God apart from dandelions and kittens, oven-fresh bread cooling on the counter, the face of your loved one reposed in sleep on the pillow beside you. All the lovely things of this earth are portraits of God who fulfills Godself in love. These portraits are creation's culmination, for everyone and everything comes into being as an emanation from the Beloved, the Creator, the Loving One.

• • •

I enter my house after having been away for a time. My feet moving across the silent floors speak in measured stanzas to the solemn chairs and tables that sit blinking in the sun. I pause before the shelves of my books, old friends that trail their shadows up the wall and often come down unseen to fill me with the hidden warmth of their companionship. I drink in the golden dust of the afternoon that sprinkles in through the spacious windows, and I put down my luggage near the old brown chair that has waited in faithful solitude to receive my frame and drain away my tiredness. I am home! I feel the ineffable wonder of welcome in all things, and in almost every ordinary object on which I rest my gaze, I find hints of God. It is for this reason that coming home always restores the hope that a sordid, despairing world tries to take. I am comfortable now. I am in my separate place. Love has already begun its renewing work. It is enough now to know that Someone knows the secret of my doors and windows, how to come in and repair the design. What remains for me is to trust each such homecoming, until I finally step over into that other House, behind which lie windows into the Forever and Ever.

• • •

There is a Hindu teaching that says that the one who perceives in his own soul the Supreme Soul in all beings, and acquires equanimity towards all, attains the highest bliss. We are in bondage and fear until we catch this great truth. To do away with all sense of separateness and to recognize the oneness of self with the Infinite, this is the spirit that breathes through all the teachings of Christ. And running through the lives of all great men and women of any age has been this same truth—union with God. This union is more deeply desired by God than it is by us. That is why God has particularized love in such a way that we would know that we have been called to be God's own. Love asks each of us to make our abiding place in God, and God then commissions us to bear the fruits of love to all the world.

•   •   •

(From the diary of an elderly woman friend, which I received after her death.)

It has come to me this evening, as I watch the day fade into twilight from my window, where now I must spend much of my time, that there is one thing in this world that is every bit as certain as night, and that is death. Death, no matter how you talk about it, is the awful abyss that removes our dear ones from us with a finality that is absolute. I do not know if there is an awakening on the other side. Perhaps there is, just as there is always day on the other side of night. I am sure I would be much comforted in these final years if I knew for sure. But this I do know. We don't have to die to go to heaven. Heaven is within us. It's not something we die for, it's something we take with us. And it's within everything. There's a Christ within all of life—every man, every bird, every tree—a quality that is sacred. It seems to me, therefore, that the worst thing we might do is not to commit some error in faith by believing the wrong thing or not believing the right thing. The worst thing we can do is mistreat someone else, for when we do, we are mistreating Christ. My voice is not heard very far these days, but if I could say anything to the world, it would simply be this: be gentle with one another. The time is short, and life is precious. Be gentle.

Love is not a dream nor an illusion. Love is the basic law of life, and we can never mature until we understand that love is the true center of life. Love is. All that is not love, is not. It is doomed to pass away, for it carries in it the seeds of its own destruction. Only love remains. All that which is, has its being and its action in love.

• • •

A young man from my church was chosen as the student speaker for his commencement. Without apology or embarrassment, he stood before that huge audience and said that the one thing in his life that had made the most difference was that each morning, as he left home to go to school, his mother would say to him, "Remember, Kevin, you are loved." That simple statement and its underlying reality became the focal point and transforming reference for his entire life.

• • •

The greatest moments in my life have not been moments when bodiless light seemed to shine on everything or ghostly voices spoke to me from the ethers. In fact, I have not had those kinds of experiences, except in rare fleeting hints within my dreams. But the greatest moments for me have been simple ones: sitting in a quiet classroom and having some bright new truth come out of a book to transform all the common things of life with some sense of unification; walking through a field of sunflowers and seeing for the first time, not with my eyes alone but with my spirit, how the sunflowers always turn their faces to follow the light; confessing to my mother when I was a child that the dark frightened me and having her come and sit by my bedside to read until I fell asleep. There are too many such moments to record; and when they came, I did not see them as great moments at all. It is only now, as I look back on life, I see that the light of love had been shining on my path all along and that I often failed to perceive when it was brightest. Perhaps what we need most is what C. S. Lewis called "a baptism of the imagination" so that we can see the commonplace of life drawn into the bright shadow of love. Thus, in such simple things as bread upon the table or embers in the fireplace we can read the marvel of life and discover anew the holiness with which God has gifted it.

• • •

The greatest idea ever to be taken up by the human mind is to be found in the teachings of Jesus Christ, for he was concerned simply and solely with love. Yet for centuries this great idea has been ignored, violated, and corrupted by his followers. Every empire built upon the sword or from the concept that might makes right has fallen victim to its own force. We have weakened our nations by building them on platforms of arrogance, independence, and belligerent strength. Now, with the development of weapons deadly enough to destroy the human race and with the advancement of suspicion and mistrust to an unprecedented high, we must face the largest order ever given to a people: to bring about a world community. Never in their fifty-odd thousand years on this earth have humans had such a tremendous assignment. But we humans have set up the conditions that make this world community necessary. We have reached the ultimatum where we must find each other in order to survive. Technology will not do it. Militarism will not do it. Tough rhetoric and saber-rattling will not do it. Nothing will do it except the ethic and precept of love as taught and exemplified by Jesus Christ.

• • •

People can lay down their lives for a cause and have it count for very little, unless their motivations are rooted in love. The blood of martyrs and terrorists alike stain the pages of history because of an obsessive commitment that was polluted with a queer mixture of self-pity and a desire for personal aggrandizement. Only those who give up their lives in selfless love perform an act of lasting and significant value. Jesus Christ voluntarily offered his life for a cause he refused to renounce, the cause of unconditional love. His service and his gift would have meant little in and of themselves. The difference came because Jesus loved. He loved humanity in such a complete and unique way that his life was united to all creation and to God as no other life had ever been. His gift in the name of an unselfish love became a victory for the world.

●　　●　　●

Do you remember to praise your child? If you don't, your child will grow up never hearing about the areas where he or she excels, the places where he or she is strong. Instead, the child only has pointed out the places where he or she is weak, the things he or she doesn't do well. You may do this under the guise of betterment, but what you are really doing is taking away from your child the possibilities of his or her own truth. Every child has a right to know that he or she does certain things well. A child has a need to be praised. A child has a desire to hear someone rejoice in the right he or she has done. Only in this way can the child respond to the art of giving praise to others, which is really the art of unconditional love.

●　　●　　●

Out of nowhere came the sun, moving easily, casually, along its own constructed highway, making a quiet valley of light out of the murky womb of the earth. It lifted the mists of a damp coast and sent me hurtling above the wash of lawns and muddy pools, back through the years, to a leafless wood where a lone man thrusts his scouring blade into the debris of last year's growing. The air is crisp, biting, its deep-drawn breath reminding chill by its misty exhalations. A haphazard pile of logs grows nearby, as the woodsman splits the remnants of trees torn loose by early storms and almost hid by huckleberry cane and rotting undergrowth. Patiently, remorselessly, he toils, ignoring the protests of aching muscles and the appearance of renewed blisters. With a single blow he cuts a tree in half, its bark in tatters, its heavy heart yielded clean to the sharp axe. The man pauses to ease the strain and wipe away the sweat from brow and eyes. The logs are stacked for carting now. One by one he loads them in the wagon and wheels them down the slope, across the meadow to the cabin. I stand beside him and watch the unpacking of the load and the rising of the stack beneath the lean-to. I do not know much of God at that point, for I am still a child, but I think God must be hid somewhere in that devoted form of man who gives up his life for me, who thinks not of himself until he knows his family is safe and warm. What greater joy exists than to fathom one phase of creation's mystery and to feel one's consciousness brought to light and given new cause by one simple act of love.

● ● ●

"Do you help Indians?" He stared at me through dark, lowered eyelids, jaws slack with the effects of too much drink. He reeked of street smells and stale beer. His clothing was rumpled and disheveled. Yet beneath the sour aroma of a deracinated civilization came the faint drift of windswept prairies, cool canyons, and fresh sage smoke, the redolence of an earlier chapter, now closed forever, but which continues to haunt us in arcane symbols and accusing memories.

"Do you help Indians?" I recoiled, not from him but from the question. Generations of broken promises, white malfeasance, and blind sophism stirred behind it. How can I answer him? How can I reach out to this son of a lost tribe with something that will replace his cubitus of sorrow with a corridor of dreams?

We need a love for the centuries, not just for the day. We need a forever love, one that can be firmly tender to its object while still permeating the harshness and bitters of the past, a love transforming all to the essence that is contributive to life, a love that will let us have another chance at advancement and hope. We need the very love of God, itself fulfilling, if we are ever to heal the famines of yesterday and bring about the larger meanings of the common soul of all humanity.

•　•　•

"Do you love me?" whispered the child anxiously, huddling her bruised and battered form shudderingly against the nurse, raising her large brown eyes imploringly, eyes that were purple-circled and reflecting a pain far too deep and pervasive for one so young. Pressing a kiss against the feather-soft cheek, the nurse replied tremulously, "Love you? Why, honey, of course I love you. I am you!"

•　•　•

Speak to us of child abusers, murderers, rapists, and other malfeasant tormentors of life. What about them? What does love do for such as these? They are the ones who give out to the world violence and fury, who leave behind a wreckage of innocent bodies broken, tender lives shattered, gentle hopes betrayed. What about love in their cases?

They are precisely as they are because love was denied to them. Somewhere along the way they missed the thing that makes the human soul grow large. They were not loved, so they do not know how to love. People are more often "sinned against" than sinners. There are those in this world whose early beginnings have so impoverished and abased them that it is necessary sometimes to lock them away from the world, in order that they will not continue to hurt others and themselves. But that locking away should not be a punitive act. It should be a loving one. It is offering to them a haven of rehabilitation, a place where some of the learning they have missed may have a chance to begin. Perhaps they will never be well enough to walk free again, but they must not be denied their right to the thing they have missed, the thing that in its absence has left them stranded on an island of their own lustful hatreds and scurrilous malevolence. Prisons should be centers for learning self-respect and respect for others, not places for instilling deeper hatreds. Those who are sent there need love, not punishment. They have already been punished. Why would we want to add more?

• • •

Some scholars of the ancient Aramaic language, in which Jesus spoke and taught, tell us that a seldom used and often overlooked meaning of the word "perfect" was "all-inclusive." If this be so, then when Jesus said, "Be perfect, as your Father in heaven is perfect," he was really telling us to be all-inclusive in our caring, to shut no one out. We all know that perfection, as a moral ideal or spiritual achievement, is something out of reach for all of us. But what about being all-inclusive? Is that also out of reach? On our own it is. But in God's grace and by God's strength, it is not. It is one of those gifts that come to us when we have inwardly demonstrated that we are ready to use it.

• • •

When Frank and Lauris had raised their children and had seen them strike out to raise families of their own, they found themselves left with a big house and open hearts. So they decided to become foster parents. The young people that came and went through their home over the next several years bore witness to the steady love that was given to them there. But none was more gratifying to Frank and Lauris than Marleen.

When Lauris first looked at Marleen, she said to herself, "If I ever learn to love this one, it will be because of God's grace and not mine." Marleen was almost grotesque. She had a narrow, pinched face, badly scarred from fresh and old acne sores, sharp features and small eyes that blinked rapidly and seldom met your own, stringy hair of some indistinguishable color that hung in greasy wisps, and a spindly form supported by unshapely legs that were matchstick thin. Her manner was hostile and furtive, almost apologetic, as though she knew she was an intrusion into a world that welcomed only beautiful people.

For several days, Marleen held herself apart. Lauris was familiar with the pattern and made no effort to intrude too quickly. The girl was not insubordinate, but she seemed disinterested in any task and equally disinterested in trying to improve her appearance. She seemed determined to be what she was, one of nature's mistakes, sullenly occupying a space until it was denied.

One night Lauris was watching television. Marleen came into the room and stood beside her chair, watching the screen but apparently not sure if she should sit down. On impulse, Lauris reached out and gave a little tug to the girl's arm. "Want to sit down and watch?" she invited. To her surprise, Marleen took it as an invitation to creep into the big chair with Lauris. When Lauris found her lap suddenly filled with a scrawny, homely sixteen-year-old girl, she did what her mother's heart prompted her to do. She wrapped both arms around her and held her close, rocking back and forth. The girl lay ever so still, savoring the warmth and welcome of the woman's generous frame. After a half hour or so, she quietly disengaged herself and went to bed.

Each night thereafter this little ritual was re-enacted. Marleen crept to Lauris's chair, and Lauris held and rocked her. It was as though the starved little heart was trying to make up for the mother love that had always been denied. This went on for several weeks. Meanwhile,

Marleen began to do her household tasks with greater energy and enthusiasm. She even took a moderate interest in her appearance, and when Lauris made her a new brightly-colored frock, her face shone with the purest pleasure.

One day Marleen announced she wanted to look for a job to earn money for college. Lauris helped her look through employment ads in the newspaper, and Marleen secured her first position as a helper at a nursing home. It was poor work, poor hours, and poor pay, but Marleen took pride in it. It was hers. She cared for the elderly patients as though they were her own children, and in their loneliness and senility, many came to see her as a gentle angel of mercy. She stayed at the job for three years, saving her money carefully, until she was able to enroll herself in college in preparation for nurse's training.

The nightly ritual of being rocked by Lauris had lasted only a few weeks, but it was enough to feed that starving portion of Marleen's psyche that had been begging for nourishment, and it was enough to help her summon enough self-confidence to declare a future for herself. When she left Lauris and Frank to be on her own, Marleen was still not beautiful. She never would be, at least in an outer sense. But she carried a new air of confidence, security and poise. She was ready now to take up arms against the world that had cruelly turned its back upon her, not by inflicting it with vengeance and reprisal, but by helping to alleviate the burdens of some of its pain-filled children. Love had done its transforming work.

●　　●　　●

Sometime when you are walking down a busy street, look quietly and unobtrusively into the face of each person you meet. Do it with a prayer of blessing in your heart for each, remembering that Christ dwells in everyone. You are sending forth your silent greeting to that divinity. Two things may begin to happen. First, you may find yourself filled alternately with joy and sorrow, joy when you discover happiness in another, sorrow when you encounter a burden. The pain and heartache dwelling in the lives of others is enough to break our hearts, if we but knew. The second thing that may happen is that someone may suddenly look up, see your face, and greet you with a smile or a warm, responsive glance. It will not be because that one knows you or wants something from you. It will be because the spirit of love in that one has recognized the spirit of love in you. In that brief moment of interchange, you are one.

• • •

When you look up into the heavens at night and contemplate the magnificence of the stars, are you conscious of your own smallness and insignificance? You ought not to be. You should be conscious of your own magnificence, your own grandeur. Those stars looking back at you cannot contemplate you, but you can contemplate them. You can comprehend them, count them, and know something about each one of them. They cannot do that for you. The human spirit is infinitely greater than all the universe, because the human spirit possesses the consciousness and love of God who created everything. Each of the stars we look at is incapable of love, but you and I are immense galaxies of love within ourselves. When we contemplate the stars in wonder and love, we become part of them. We are communing with them and communing with ourselves at the same time, until the magnitude of our very self is melted into the magnitude of the heavens. Our bodies are made up of the same chemical elements as the stars, so the universe is literally our own flesh. In such realizations, we are touching all creation with a holy word of love, and that love becomes incarnate in the universe.

• • •

I had been reading intermittently while listening to the storm. I looked out the window, watching the wind bend and shake the camellia bushes. The sound of splashing rain diminished as the downpour gave way to a mild drizzle. I put my head against the back of the chair and drowsed, passing across the threshold of a gentle dream where the symphony of wind and rain mingled in soft confusion with some solemn, redemptive strain of music. I must have dozed only a few minutes, when suddenly I felt a movement against my mind, a moment's gentle tracery as light and delicate as a cobweb but which startled me into wakefulness as though someone had shouted at me. I opened my eyes and, looking out the window, the camellia bushes were quiet. The rain had stopped, the wind had died down. Everything was silent with an ominous portent that seemed to grip the air. All creation was waiting, as though preparing to accept into the next moment either an outrending anguish or a white blaze of joy. A muffled crack of thunder from some distant peak broke like the rolling of drums. Someone is coming, I thought. But who? What?

I watched, yet no figure moved across the gray landscape of my window pane. My eyes sought and identified again the blurred but totally familiar backdrop of trees and sky. I found again the shuddering camellia bushes that framed the window. I did not move. I had a premonition that someone was coming to my door. I listened carefully, but there was no sound of feet scraping softly against the steps leading to the front door nor of shoes being wiped carefully on the mat. The morning minutes crept by as I waited, bemused in emotions that bordered on apocalyptic excitement. Yet still no one came. Nothing happened. Eventually I picked up my book and resumed reading.

What mean such moments as these? Is this how death arrives, a shrouded visitor prowling through rainy streets who comes to one's door at the moment the storm ceases and then decides its arrival is premature so departs? Or could it be an old friend trying to move to us from the other side but unable to pierce fully the veil that separates our knowing? Or, best of all, could it be God, making known a silent, invisible presence in such a way that our hearts are made forever alert to any possible breakthrough of love? Is this how grace comes, I wonder? We sense its approach, not as a living terror but as a saintly, compassionate friend at the end of a storm, yet so unobtrusive is its entrance we do not even know we have been given a gift. Then comes the opportunity to use it, and suddenly we discover we have love we had not even thought possible.

•　•　•

When we love another person, we are really sharing a gift that is the very substance of God. Our union with another is only possible because of our union with the divine. That's why God's love is unselfish; it is lavished abundantly on any and all, and seeks the unified expression of love between two persons in love. As long as our love is free from selfishness, it is the kind of love which is also God.

•　•　•

For about an hour before the storm broke, the sky to the north had loomed in ominous black cloud patterns over our heads. When the rain started, it became as dark as a tomb inside the schoolroom, and we could no longer see to read or write. Though it was early afternoon, the teacher dismissed school, for by now the rain was reducing the snow banks to puddles and causing rivulets of brown water to run everywhere. "Go straight home as fast as you can," she warned.

I headed old Diamond onto the road, but he seemed less inclined to gallop that homeward trail than usual. The storm bewildered him, made him thrust his ears forward sharply and whistle shrilly through his nose. The borrow pits beside the road were now running full, and for the first time in many months the road, previously packed with snow, was showing its pebbled soil bed. Although it was not yet three o'clock, it was like twilight. The entire countryside was enshrouded in a watery gloom that made familiar objects along the road nearly indistinguishable. I gave Diamond his head and trusted he would stay in the middle of the road.

We came to the bridge where the waters of the Little Lost River cross under the roadway to make their way to the lower valley. I recognized the tall gray cottonwoods that stand as sentinels at this point. Diamond stopped and snorted. I urged him forward, kicking him gently in the ribs. He took a few steps, stopped again, and refused to go farther, no matter how vigorously I urged him. I could not see ahead, but I heard, above the furious pounding of rain, the roar of swirling waters. The river had flooded its banks and was rushing over the top of the bridge. The horse refused to attempt the crossing, and there was no alternative but to go back and take the longer road that led home along the back of the fields.

It was an hour later before we finally came to the place where the road branched off to the house. It was steadily growing darker, and I was drenched and shivering. Anxiously I strained my eyes through the inky dusk in an attempt to glimpse the house or barns. Then I saw it. Piercing its way through the mist of the premature night shone the light from the kitchen window. Even as I watched, the light flickered and seemed to go out, then came back on. It did this for several times, and I realized someone was pacing back and forth in front of the window, looking out into the gloom to see if I was coming. I knew it was my mother. She was waiting for me, caring for me, anxious for my homecoming. The thought of her loving concern filled me with a sense of well-being and gratitude, as I spurred old Diamond into the yard.

Many years after that storm, my wife and I drove from California to Idaho to visit my family. We were delayed by another storm, during which the image of my mother waiting for me when I was a little boy renewed itself in my mind. When we at last drove into the yard, she was again at the window, anxiously anticipating our arrival. Even after all these years, her heart of love waits for her child, now grown, to come home. How strange that I should reach so far to find the tools of what I am, when all that is or was or ever shall be for me is secured somehow in that loving, sturdy soul, who has so often yielded her life for her children and has molded her destiny to enhance their own. There is really only one lesson to learn in life, and that is the lesson of love. Mother helped teach me that lesson by showing me in a thousand different ways what love means. Most of all, she loved me long before I even knew what love was all about.

●　●　●

Unconditional love at its peak is the embracing of every experience, of every thing, of every one, with the whole heart. But it has to begin small, with just a few, and move out from there, till ultimately it reaches the universe.

●　●　●

From the Zen Buddhist Master Chuang Tzu comes this thought: "Suppose a boat is crossing a river, and another boat, an empty one, is about to collide with it. Even an irritable man would not lose his temper. But suppose there was someone in the second boat. Then the occupant of the first would shout to him to keep clear. And if he did not hear him the first time, nor even when called to three times, bad language would inevitably follow. In the first case there was no anger because the boat was empty. In the second case there was anger because the boat was occupied. So it is with man. If he could only pass empty through life, who would be able to injure him?"

In the manner of Christ we are asked to empty ourselves, not to erase people or pretend they are not there, nor to erase ourselves, but to share with others the love God has lavished upon us. Unconditional love requires an empty vessel. When it is there, you are not.

● ● ●

There is a lot of stirring today for a return to the Bible, a return to basics, a return to true Christianity. We don't need a return to Christianity, if by that we mean that complex of doctrines, organizations, liturgies, traditions, and social habits, all of which are largely human-made. We need a return to faith in a personal commitment to Jesus Christ as the exemplar of holy love. We need a return to unconditional love. Complete fullness of life for all of us will be a love relationship with everyone, in which we depend on others and at the same time give to others. We need a return to that. When that happens, we will evoke God's greatest pleasure.

● ● ●

My father was a miner. He spent most of his life prospecting for gold in the Little Lost River Mountains of Idaho. He never found the bonanza that would have made him wealthy. In fact, he was poor all his life and died penniless. But he got to do what he wanted to; he got to live the way he wanted. And he taught me something I will never forget. In mining, one always looks for the lode vein of mineral deposits, that somewhat continuous unstratified metal-bearing vein, which is the source of all the smaller veins or deposits. A true prospector is never satisfied with just a few nuggets or deposits of gold dust. He always looks for the source. It is no less true in the spiritual life. God is the lode vein, the source of all other forms of life. Why settle for a few grains of dust, when God has promised a bonanza, a kingdom, to those who will unite their lives in love to him?

● ● ●

When we call something holy we really mean that God has placed a mark upon it that speaks of love. One holy place from my early life was the kitchen table. It was covered with oilcloth of some arcane design, faded and scrubbed beyond definition. In the center, certain things usually remained from meal to meal: salt and pepper shakers, a sugar jar, a little holder of toothpicks, and a large ornate glass full of spoons. The table was not only the place where we met for physical nourishment, it was the place where I worked my arithmetic lessons by the light of a kerosene lantern. It was the place where Mother read to us, often a chapter or two of some old story before bedtime. It was the place where we played games of Chinese checkers or hangman's knot. It was the place where we matched strength against one another in arm wrestling. It was the place where ranch work was plotted and fishing trips of the past embellished and adorned. It was the place where Mother spread out a bolt of fresh material to cut the design for an apron or a dress. It was the place where our lives came together as a family in a thousand different ways. It was, without my ever knowing it then, a holy place where God sent his love and established a foundation on which we might build our lives.

● ● ●

There is a wooded ravine behind our house in Seattle, through which flows a tiny creek. Sometimes at night we hear the lonely cries of the coyotes who live in that ravine. They are wild animals who have been caught by the encroachment of human civilization and who, while accommodating to it, continue to live in alienation from it. Their cries always take me back across the years to another place, an old farmhouse in a snowy valley. Lying in bed at night, buried under piles of blankets, warming my feet on a flat iron wrapped in flannel, I would listen to the mournful wails of coyote packs coming across the frozen fields and plains and feel a lonely piece in my own life rise up in communion.

The coyote was free then. Today in many places its freedom is fading, giving way to the relentless urbanization of the wilderness. This modern entrapment of the coyote is a parable of our own time. Our lives have changed drastically and conclusively. Our children will never live as we have lived, and they will accomplish things our minds can only dimly comprehend. Yet in the midst of our excitement comes the lonely cry of a lost humanity that stands at the end of an age, the age of human reason, not knowing where to go. We have tried to accommodate to the times, and still we stand strangely alienated from them.

Our problem is partly because we are a transition people, living between the death of one age and the birth of another. But our problem is also because we are on this earth in exile from our true Source and our true being. Our yearning cries, like those of the coyote, are for God, and we are forever lost and lonely until we have joined our lives to God. Then our age will unfold to reveal its own destined wonders.

• • •

Sometimes we wonder if we shall ever heal the breaches and disruptions that hold the human family apart. We wonder if love without conditions can ever be true for us. An image comes to me from my childhood which alleviates such despair. One day, when my cousin Ted and I were not much more than ten years old, we decided to "borrow" the family pick-up and go for a drive by ourselves. We had no business doing such a thing, because neither of us knew much about driving. He was a bit more advanced than I and had promised to give me instructions that would improve my limited capacity as a driver. Only by sitting on the extreme edge of the seat could our short legs reach the clutch, the brake, and the accelerator. And only by peering through the steering wheel instead of over it could we see where we were going. In spite of such handicaps we managed to drive that truck down the dusty road along the river to the hay field. There we practiced all the rudiments of driving across furrowed rows and rutted stubble fields. Riding a roller coaster would have been infinitely easier than riding that old truck across those bumps and ruts, accompanied by the grinding of gears, the too sudden release of the clutch and the too sudden depression of the accelerator. Nevertheless, we shot around that field in erratic and peripatetic patterns, giddy with pleasure and excitement. How long this might have continued I cannot say, for suddenly the pick-up coughed to a stop. It was out of gas.

We contemplated fleeing from the scene and pretending ignorance as to how the truck got into the field. But we decided a better course might be to push it back up the road to the place in the yard where we had found it. It was no easy task for two puny little boys to push that monstrous old vehicle back across those stubbled rows. When I, the more faint-hearted of the two, would stop to rest and complain over what seemed an impossible task, my resourceful cousin would say, "But look back and see how far we've already come!" As I considered the distance already covered, I would take fresh heart, and once again we would unite efforts to push the truck homeward. Unfortunately, we practically rolled it over my stepfather, who was striding briskly down the road in our direction, having witnessed our little escapade from the top of the barn, where he had been repairing the roof.

Something in that image of two errant little boys, pushing a truck much too big for their strength, is parallel with where we are today in our world. But we must take inventory of what we have achieved. We must look back and see how far we have already come. It will give us heart to go on and accomplish an unprecedented destiny—the miracle of healing the fragmented body of our humanity by bringing together in love all the precious people of this wonderful planet. See how far we've already come! In spite of all our problems and diversities, we have never been closer to one another and closer to the kingdom of love than we are at this very moment.

• • •

I stood on a mountain peak and watched an eagle soar in the valley below me. Buoyed by the currents of air that seemed to cradle him in tender embrace, the eagle did not even move its wings. His secret is this: he locks his wings, picks up the thermals, and rides the winds. He literally floats in the arms of the universe. For a fleeting moment, I, who was higher than he from my vantage point, felt myself cradled in the same infinite love that held the eagle. It was God, giving me a glimpse of myself, showing me that my true life is held in invisible arms of holy love.

• • •

From the literature of the Desert Fathers comes the story of three men who came to Abba Achilles and asked him to make them a fishing net. Abba Achilles refused the first two men, telling them he did not have time. But he agreed to make a fishing net for the third, a man who had a bad reputation. The first two men felt slighted and later asked Abba Achilles why he would not make a net for them. The old man answered, "I told you I did not have time, and you understood. You were not disappointed and our fellowship was not broken. But the third man is burdened with great sin. If I had told him no, it would have added more to the burden he already carries. He would have thought I was refusing him because of his sin, and our relationship would have broken down. But now I have cheered his soul, and he will not be overcome with grief."

Unconditional love always takes note of the conditions in life that make others what they are. It seeks to lift burdens rather than adding them. It does more than understand; it actually *stands under* as a supporting presence.

• • •

There is an abiding desire in all of us to be loved. Even when we say we do not care about this person and that, when we declare it does not matter what others think, the insistence still remains—we want to be loved. This yearning is a part of the anxiety we all face at every moment of our lives. If we could be sure that there will always be someone who will love us, who will not betray us and leave us abandoned in some lonely place, then we would know the peace that passes understanding. But life is never quite like that. Receiving love is never a thing apart from our ability to give love.

We bring into our search for love all the love that has nourished us in the past, as well as all the love denied to us. To find the love we yearn for, we must be able to summon the courage to step out on life's beckoning way and let the universe have another fling with our emotions. Love is forever. It is not lost, even where hurt, shame, anger, resentment or hate are felt. Stirred by the bitterness of heart and mind that gather poisons unto themselves, love continues to permeate, continues to impress, continues to demand.

The best thing that can happen to us is to remember that the significance of anything lies in a reality beyond, a reality that transcends these yearning days of human existence. Our desire to be loved is nothing more than our desire for God, and it will not pass, not even when we are lying safe and secure in the arms of a lover. Love is forever. Its yearning hunger does not go away. Only in God does the restless longing, the insistent searching, begin to diminish. Only in God can we find the love which all our lives we have yearned for and sought.

● ● ●

Love goes beyond all rules, but the sage, who would sum it up in a single prescription, might suggest these three principles: accept what comes, do not cling, listen to your heart. Or it might be put another way: delete your need to understand, learn to let go, and honor your inner guidance. Still another way might be: don't make comparisons, take what comes without fuss, and be true to yourself. There is always the need for gentle detachment from the object of your love, and there is always reason to remember that love has not the right to ask for self-subjugation. When you can keep some sort of balancing wisdom around love, you can trust it and know it will not hurt you beyond your ability to repair and mend.

●   ●   ●

These delicious mornings, when I stay home to write, impress and intoxicate with an indescribable sense of well-being. Soft hours glide by and lure me from my desk out to the bluff, where I sit in contemplation, beguiled by sea breezes, dissolved in sunbeams, and immersed in contentment. The sailboats are like huge swans swimming on a golden pond. A wild bird drops an exhilarating note on me as it soars to a dead branch jutting from a pine tree. I decide I will not cut off that branch after all, since he seems to like sitting there. The whole atmosphere offers limpid peace, luminous splendor and groundless space. The infinite has entered the finite with a kind of numen.

The weather report says that tomorrow this same spot will be invaded by storm, an invasion that will bring an oppressive effect and strip away all the layers of serenity. The water will toss its waves angrily, like white manes on the backs of rebellious horses. The wind and rain will join hands in a wild, wrenching race through the sky. And few creatures will dare stir or defy. We must learn to live with the contradictions, to accept the unacceptable, to move from serenity to confusion. The world is a funny place that only makes sense to those who love it. It is a constantly changing place. I have elected to make love my constant support and to look for the same splendor in a storm that I find in a sunny day.

●   ●   ●

They tell us there is a feminine style of ego consciousness, an attitude that accepts life as it is, without
power-motivated ambition or blind sentimentality. It is a
style that does not endorse, or condone, or appropriate, or
even try to change—it just accepts what is. In this style
one need not identify with or detach from; one simply
accepts who and what the other is. This is not passive, it is
the most energetic inward action of which the soul is capable. I wonder then why there is a resistance to the
feminist movement? Why should we detest that which
would help us achieve soul greatness? Would it not mean
liberation for everyone if we could reach such a pure response of life to life?

● ● ●

There is a spot on the creek where part of the stream
is diverted to a narrow channel between rocks. Here it
flows with considerable force and energy, like an unruly
child suddenly released from the constraints of a school
room. A spider had built her web across that rock-walled
channel. Even as I watched her toil to strengthen the
fragile filament, a sudden rush of water, splashing
against the rocks, hit the web and carried it away. With
infinite patience, the spider reconstructed the web, a
miracle work that took but a few seconds. Then came another watery burst, and the web was gone. I marveled at
the spider's persistence in rebuilding its web each time it
was destroyed, but my critical self decided that the spider
might have chosen a better spot. It was easy to see she had
made a hard selection. Still she continued. Each time her
web was broken must have been a dark moment, but it did
not deter her from patiently flinging another strand
across the narrow chasm. Each failure only seemed to
make the spider more determined to succeed.

It is an easy matter to look at the circumstances of
another person's life and make our judgments about what
is wrong and why. But who gave the onlooker such
options? What is finally important is not what decisions

are made but whether the strength that is available is being rightly appropriated to work with the decisions. Struggle, even in the face of uneven odds can be a steppingstone to greatness. No one has the vision to understand fully the circumstances in another's life nor to know what forces impel particular choices. We who sit in our safe place and note the course that others have taken have only one assignment—*love*. Drop all judgments. They only make the struggle harder.

•   •   •

I would like to be honest with you. I would like to take off all the masks, strip away all the layers, dispense with all protective shields, and let you see the real me. But I am terrified to do this. I am afraid you will not want to be around me if I do.

Is your love truly unconditional? Will you still love me if you discover I have a little sewer of thoughts and fantasies I have never let anyone see? Will you love me if you realize that I am not nearly as poised and self-confident as I pretend to be? Will you love me if you see that many times I am closer to failure than I am to success? Will you love me if you discover my instinctive selfishness, my undisciplined dreams, my ambiguous motives, my hidden terrors?

I want to be my highest self, and yet hurts and fears cause me to judge and block the flow of love. Will you please be kind to me and not judge me back? I know that God has given me an inner love to set me free. But I need you to nurture me along that path of love's fulfillment. If you will do it for me, I will do the same for you. Together, perhaps we can be love's fulfillment to each other.

•   •   •

I know why I don't want to be with him. He always tries to control me. He is constantly saying to me, "You ought to do this; you must do that; here's what you really need," etc. And I become annoyed and fearful that if I do all those things I will abdicate the rule of my life into his hands. He is not that way with me alone. In every situation where I have observed him, he attempts to dominate and direct the flow of events. I have noticed he has almost no friends that stay with him very long, and here I am (one of his best, he tells me), considering drawing away. Yet he needs me. He needs someone who will listen to him when he talks about the sorrow he is having with his son, now estranged from him, the sense of frustration he feels with his business, the uncertainties that plague him about religion and matters of faith. If I abandon him, who will he have?

Yet what does he have now? I am not really his friend because I don't like him the way he is. I pity him, but that's not a basis for friendship. If I were more honestly concerned about him, I would share with him what I am feeling. Then I would search for a way to demonstrate unconditional love, to let him know I am not pulling back, that I am looking for a place in our relationship where I can be free and honest. If he cannot accept that, then the friendship, such as it is, may have to end. But would it not be better to have an honest relationship than one that is totally dominated by another and causes such suppressed anger?

Today his wife told me he is an exact replica of his parents. He was never allowed to make decisions for himself when he was growing up. They knew what he needed and made all his choices for him. He bent to their control as long as he was at home, but when he left, he established the very patterns of dominance in his own behavior that he had so deplored in his parents. He became the thing he hated, because he didn't know a better way.

When I heard that, I felt I understood him for the first time. To understand all is to forgive all. To forgive all is to love unconditionally. If I can truly embrace unconditional love, with its requirement of non-control, and model this for him, perhaps I can offer him a climate where he will begin to assimilate it into his own life. It's worth trying.

• • •

They think they know where the monarch butterfly goes each fall. This tiny fragment of life, with only one winter to live, always vanishes when winter comes, flying south to some unknown destiny and then returning to its summer breeding grounds when winter is over. Now that elusive wintering place has been discovered in the Sierra Madre Mountains, northwest of Mexico City. The conclusion of zoologists is that the monarch butterfly originated there, far back in geologic time, and each winter returns to a place it has never seen before through some instinct or programming that we don't fully know or understand. There it mates in temperatures just below freezing, an environment perfectly suited for its semi-dormant state where it will not burn up any reserve fat. In the spring, it will start its incredible journey back to the northland, where it will lay its eggs before dying.

But the mystery is not completely cleared up. How can such a fragile, wind-tossed scrap of life find its way (only once!) across uncharted prairies, deserts, mountains, valleys, even cities, to that remote pinpoint, there to mate and await some mysterious signal, probably the angle of light from the ascending sun, that will trigger the north-bound migration flight back across those same prairies, deserts, mountains, and valleys? As they like to say nowadays, "It boggles the mind."

The plan for the butterfly was written by the same God who created you and me. We are linked to the butterfly by a common Creator, who has a similar plan for both of us. The butterfly has no option about agreeing to its plan, so far as we can tell. The plan for its life is an inseparable part of its being. The plan for our lives is also an inseparable part of our being, but we have the option of disagreeing with it if we choose. The results are tragic if we do; yet even when we agree, the struggle is not over. We too must make a journey across uncharted continents and untrodden territories. Like the tiny butterfly, we must commit ourselves to that infinite ocean of air where there are no familiar landmarks, nothing but a kind of glory that lights up our minds and helps us migrate back to our Source. We humans are migratory creatures too. We may place our bodies in the same locale for years, but our spirits are always being urged to launch out with adventurous hope on a thousand or more journeys a day. We are always in quest of the infinite, drawn by that yearning hunger for connection to the homeland of our being. We are not driven by fear; we are drawn by love. And love will bring us home.

•　•　•

She has been beside me for more than two decades now. When she is away for some reason, I miss her more than I am ever able to put into words. She has stood beside me through all my moods, my yearnings, my victories, my defeats. She has seen me at my worst, and she has also seen me at my best. She has never stopped believing in me, even when I was bound in some pit of discouragement and defeat. She, more than any other, has shown me unconditional love. She has made me believe in it, not by words or precepts but by her steady, unwavering example. If one person can do that for us, it frees us to be what indeed we are: God's word of love to the universe. Without Beverly, my wife, this book could never have been written, for without her I would never have discovered the deeper reality of love without conditions.

•　•　•

Evening has come. In a few minutes I shall rise and light the lamps against the growing darkness. Let me sit a moment longer and bask in this gentle transition of day into night. Twilight is a land of few words. It needs no language, so I shall give it none. Yet as the eagle rests upon the air, as a swimmer floats in the water, as the butterfly trusts the invisible charts of the journey, I would learn to lean back, to relax into the deep embrace of God, to know that no effort of mine can ever hope to earn this all-surrounding love and that no effort of mine can ever destroy it. There is no need then for anything but a final commitment:

Loving One, Thank you for your love, unfathomable in its origin, timeless in its sweep, transforming in its essence. Let me go on and on, deeper and deeper, into your love, until I am fully one with you and your creations, even as you are now fully one with me. Amen.

●　　●　　●

Unconditional Love

Unconditional love.
A fearful thing to write,
An awesome thing to contemplate.
Unconditional—meaning
Without merit, without qualification,
Even without reason, at least as we know it.
Love—meaning
The desire to embrace the whole,
The resolve to bruise nothing,
To bless the all with my all,
The active effort to see the good in everything.

Love asks for the total surrender of my being
Into the allness of God,
That I might come to that place
Where I treat others as I wish to be treated,
As God treats me.

To say, "I love," is true to the moment,
But less than true—much less.
To say, "I am loved," is true to time,
But still falls short of truth.
To say, "I am loved unconditionally,"
Is true to eternity,
And is to grow into love's likeness.

I find myself again and again reassembled,
Given new life, new strength, new goals,
As my love moves from self-determination

To self-fulfillment and beyond,
To self-offering, where love is given as freely
As it is offered by Creator to creation.
In love we live and move and have our being.
Love is why we are here,
And love is what we are to become:
Love without limits,
Love without conditions.

—Rodney Romney